W9-BMA-645

NEW BEGINNINGS
A PASTORATE
START UP WORKBOOK

ROY M. OSWALD

AN ALBAN INSTITUTE PUBLICATION

The Publications Program of The Alban Institute is assisted by a grant from Trinity Church, New York City.

ISBN #1-56699-032-7

CONTENTS

If you have moved or are about to move into a new parish ministry, this workbook is for you. It is designed to guide you through that very special period that exists for the first 18 months of every ministry. It is written so as to meet you at the point of entry—when you are entering new roles, entering new relationships, entering new phases of your career.

We suspect that many ministries have been seriously hindered because the pastor and the parish did not get off to a good start. The first twelve months will set the tone for your entire ministry in your new parish. What gets set in motion in these opening months will have a far-reaching effect. For these reasons, I encourage you to be aware and intentional about your start-up style.

We think the church has been remiss in its ministry to parish clergy by assuming that transitions from one parish to another are no big deal. "Clergy have been making these transitions for years—why think it's anything special?"

... thereby offering no training to parish clergy at the time of transition,
... and offering only minimal support and guidance as the transition evolves.

Each pastorate start up should be viewed as "a dangerous opportunity." Though the transition waterway is strewn with rocks and shoals, potential opportunities abound downriver. We want church professionals to be supported and guided into moving with the current. With that guidance and support, they can tap into new sources of energy without risking personal hurt and political wounds in the process.

Before you begin working with this workbook, we encourage

you to read our first attempt to put our reseach findings into print—the monograph, *The Pastor As Newcomer* (Alban Institute, 1977). Some of the designed experiences in this book are based on our research.

Where possible, we encourage you to go through this workbook with some colleagues who are also in transitional situations. Your learnings will be enhanced considerably if you can combine your personal insights with direct feedback from peers who share your situation. If at all possible, hire a consultant to work with you (someone with some skills in experiential education and familiarity with the parish ministry).

You face an important time in your clergy career. It is a very special time of learning, of being alive, of encountering new experiences, yet grieving over the loss of other experiences. It is worth setting aside some time for yourself to reflect on your past ministry in a disciplined fashion, so you won't continue to perpetuate past shortcomings. Nothing much in your ministry will change unless you decide to make it change. Most of us continue in familiar patterns of behavior because our fear of experimenting with new behaviors is greater than our fear of facing the consequences of old mistakes. But it need not be so.

The transition you face could mark a turning point in your ministry, a time when you learn how to get even more kicks out of being a parish pastor.

So . . .

. . . slow down

. . . take some time out for yourself.

Use the exercises in the book to fullest advantage by giving each one the time and psychological space it needs to allow insights to emerge that could be helpful to you and your new ministry. Remember, this is a workbook, not something you read through in one sitting. When you come to a stop sign at the end of sections, really stop and do some reflective writing or sharing with colleagues.

If you have not yet terminated with your former parish, we strongly recommend utilizing the monograph *Running Through the Thistles* (Alban Institute, 1978). In order to start up well you need to have terminated well. This book will guide you through a thorough termination process.

We also highly recommend one other publication—*Religious Authenticity in the Clergy* (Alban Institute, 1975) by John Fletcher. In it John describes three crises through which clergy, in relationship with laity, come to be authenticated as religious leaders of their congregations.

If, in your use of this book, you or a group discover new insights related to pastorate start ups, write them down and share them with us. We desire to be the conduit through which insights on clergy start ups can be passed on to others. Updates on our projects frequently are covered in *Action Information*, the Alban Institute's bi-monthly journal. Your insights and those of others can be shared through this medium. So let's hear from you.

Have a good time with this workbook. We've had many great experiences working through these designs with parish clergy in some of our Pastorate Start Up Seminars.

CHAPTER I

Easing the Transition— Giving Yourself Space

During a transition, both clergy and parishioners experience the inevitable stress that change brings. Some of their experiences will be quite similar; others will be quite different. For example, both will feel the grief of leaving and both will experience the strangeness and the excitement of starting up. Yet, the two groups will probably have quite different experiences during the interim period between the departure of one pastor and the arrival of another.

Congregations normally experience a long interim period—an average of nine to twelve months. At best, some clergy take a month's vacation between pastorates. Most, however, preach their farewell sermon on one Sunday and preach their start-up sermon in the new congregation the following Sunday. For them there is virtually no interim period.

I am aware of several clergy who decided to approach the interim in a more intentional and healthy way. One clergyman in Ohio, who attended a "transition awareness event" sponsored by the national office of his denomination, spent his first Sunday in his new congregation sitting in the pew. The congregation had arranged to give him the Sunday off to help him get settled into his new home. Another clergyman not only took his regular month's vacation between pastorates but was allowed a month's transition time for himself and his family. They spent the first month getting settled into a new home and community and the second at a lakeside cottage. He talked about how important that interim period was for him and his family:

> We had a lot of things to talk about—what it was like saying goodbye to the congregation—what our stay there had meant to us—some of the hopes and dreams that had to be let go. We also discussed the future as a family in a new place—what

things we wanted to do differently this time—what things would be important for us to continue as a family. The month went very quickly. When it was over, we were ready to begin ministry in the new parish.

I urge you to give yourself this kind of space as you move from one parish to another. It will make a big difference in how you start up your ministry.

CHAPTER II

Celebrating with the Search Committee

Just as congregations often fail to recognize the trauma clergy and their families experience when making a transition from one community to another, new pastors often fail to realize the effort a search committee has expended trying to find a good match for the parish.

Rarely are those who serve on a search committee warned of the complexity of the task or the long, hard hours that will be required. Ninety-five percent of search committee members have never taken on such a job before, and most will never do it again. Just this one time, they give a "pound of flesh" to their congregations.

This is not to say that the task lacks stimulation and excitement. That element is what draws people ever deeper into the task—and to more and longer meetings. Participants generally become deeply enmeshed in each other's lives, and when their task is over, they may miss the excitement and the deep involvement. Yet this grief and feeling of separation rarely is dealt with in any intentional way.

Because you are the end-product of the committee's work, you will find this small group of people highly invested in your doing well. Each member harbors a secret hope that you will walk on water and bring such energy and vitality to the parish that they will have to hold people back at the door. (They may not admit this openly, but they all hope they will be remembered as the group that made a super choice for the parish.)

If you're aware that they want you to do well, you may be tempted to dive right in and start working your magic. Before you do, however, it would be well for you to spend some time with this search committee. You may feel strange being the one who begins to debrief them on their task, but in many ways, it is quite appropriate for you to do so. Search committee members often feel burned out and exploited by the congregation; they don't feel genuinely appreciated for their work. You can help soothe these wounds, and in so doing, move from being their candidate to being their pastor.

This group also needs to celebrate the completion of their task. It would be quite appropriate for you to suggest that they plan some kind of event with you that will culminate their work together. You may or may not decide to invite other members of the congregation to join you.

For your own sake, as well, you need to take time to celebrate the significance of the process that has ended. You have just come through a negotiation period with a new congregation. You have committed yourself to a move and a period of time within a new community. Now it's time to celebrate.

Generally, we church folk do not take enough time to celebrate in our midst the reaching of goals or the completion of tasks. Driven as we are, we simply get on with the next task without stopping to say: "Hey, we really did this!"

So enjoy!

CHAPTER III

Termination Emotions

Self

Beginning your ministry in a new parish? Eager to tear right in and get things moving? Before you get into planning and doing, take a minute to be in touch with yourself. All of us tend to underestimate the impact that transitions have on us. In what kind of shape did your transition leave you?

Take a deep breath—and be quiet for a moment. Center in on the kinds of feelings floating around inside of you.

—Are there things and people you miss from your last place?
—What's left unresolved?
—Do you find yourself denying your feelings about leaving?
—Do you feel any guilt for having left your last place?
—Any anger?
—At whom?
—And why?

In deciding to move, did you make any bargains with yourself—with your family—with God?

What will it take to gain resolution on some of these issues?

Take a minute now to rate yourself as to the kind of emotional state you are in. Perhaps the rating will force you to struggle to get in closer touch with where you are.

1. Upset and distraught
2. Feeling the pain of termination but managing
3. Coping with a variety of loose ends but feeling okay
4. Basically in good shape but with twinges of loss and pain for the old situation

5. Being excited and exuberant about the new situation with no feeling of loss

If the rating helped you identify more clearly where you are, and you discover a residue of unresolved feelings, take a minute to brainstorm what you might do about that.

Here are some possibilities:

—Ignore it
—Share it with your spouse
—Talk it over with your judicatory executive
—Telephone someone in your old situation
—Go visit a friend and talk it through

We would recommend that you seek out some other person you trust and talk through some of the things you are feeling. Ask this other person to simply listen or to help you probe more deeply for the roots of those feelings. Your brainstorming list may reveal to you who that "other" might be. We do hope you take seriously your unresolved feelings about terminating another situation. Remember the Lone Ranger of Radioland from long ago? He left in a cloud of dust before people could thank him for all the wonderful things he had done for them. He is the epitome of American stoicism. We believe there are some serious liabilities to functioning that way in the parish ministry. It requires one to sit on some powerful feelings and pretend they are not there.

Unfortunately, you can't make feelings go away that easily. These emotions will emerge inappropriately and possibly jeopardize your new ministry. If you take time now to deal with those feelings directly, you will be clearing the deck for a fresh start in a new place. You owe it to yourself, your family and your new parish.

So, slow down.
Be gentle with yourself and your feelings.
Be fully in touch with them.
Seek out some pastoral help to assist you in dealing with them.
Begin to seek out a support system for yourself in this new place.
Begin with the one or two folks who have the capacity to understand what is happening to you.
Don't be afraid to ask them for some time just to help you stay in touch with what is happening . . .
psychologically,
spiritually,

physically,
... during these early months of ministry.

Remember what St. Paul said about his strength being made perfect in weakness. At this stage of your ministry, your strength will come as you get fully in touch with your weakness and vulnerability. You will gain respect by seeking out the resources you need to be fully human, here and now.

Family *(Single clergy may want to skip this section.)*

As you begin in your new parish, it is important that you take care of yourself first. You'll receive all kinds of invitations *not* to take care of yourself and to be dependent upon others in the parish. Building a support system for yourself within the parish is important, but don't fall into the trap of thinking that others will take care of you in this new situation. After you have become clear about what you need in order to be fully human in this new situation and have begun to seek out that kind of assistance, it is important to look seriously at how your spouse and family are handling the transition. After all, they are your primary support system. You will find it difficult to function effectively if they continue to have difficulty adjusting.

Clergy generally adjust to a new situation far more quickly than their families. Clergy can jump right in and immediately become immersed in work and relationships. Spouses and children must find support through more subtle and less directed ways. While you are reveling in the new situation, you may come home to persons who are hiding their tears or stifling their resentment about having to leave the old place. Take a minute now to think through how you might be more fully supportive of them in this transition.

—Where will you find the extra time to be with them during these initial months?
—Are you able to be with them as they make some initial entries into new groups or situations?
—What will you need to do in order to stay in touch with what they are going through or feeling?
—What are the family rituals that you need to be sure to continue from your last place?
—Are you able to see to it that they have the opportunity to be in touch with old friends again?

—In the midst of change and confusion, what can you do to
bring order, stability, and familiarity to your family setting?

Pastor's families often get the least pastoral attention. Is it possible at this time of transition for you to seek some outside pastoral
care for your spouse and family? If the problem gets serious, are
you able to enter counseling as a family with a family therapist?

When we're under pressure, we tend to be most demanding of
those we love. You are under a good deal of pressure now to prove
yourself in this new situation. You'll be tempted to let concerns for
spouse and family slide during this time. Don't do it. It is important
that your spouse and family remain high on your list of people who
receive your attention and energy. Your new parish has survived
this long without you—for the moment they will continue to be
okay. Your significant others don't have the resources your parish
has to draw upon during this special time of transition.

By taking care of yourself and your family you will be laying two
important foundation blocks as you build toward a significant ministry in this new place.

The Parish

Just as you and your family are going through a major transition, so
is your new parish. More than likely a huge residue of feelings remains around the termination of your predecessor.

To assume that the mere passage of time between that termination and your arrival will adequately dispel those feelings is to
make a serious mistake. Even if the majority of people did not like
your predecessor, there will still be unresolved feelings to deal
with. Parishioners may have some feelings of anger toward the former pastor that remain unresolved or some feelings of guilt about
how they treated him/her or concerning the circumstances of his/
her leaving.

The parish needs real pastoral care as people try to resolve their
feelings about your predecessor. You may be required to listen to
the same old stories about the former pastor over and over again. It
is important that you neither stifle the expression of these feelings
nor become concerned that parishioners seem to be comparing
you to their former pastor. They are simply trying to resolve powerful feelings so they can get on with their relationship with you.

So, if the expressions about the former pastor are negative, try
to listen without participating in running down her/him. If the ex-

pressions are positive, try to affirm the ministry of your predecessor without feeling threatened or put down.

Richard Kirk, in his publication, *On the Calling and Care of Pastors* (Alban Institute, 1973), postulates that a congregation will go through the same stages of grief that an individual goes through in dealing with the death or loss of a loved one. This would imply that your new congregation may be going through any of the following stages: denial, anger, guilt, or bargaining.

You should be alert to symptoms of grief within the congregation. Parishioners may be going through one or two of these stages right now. You may encounter anger that seems inappropriately directed at you. This happened some years ago at St. Mark's Capitol Hill in Washington, D.C.* After only a few months at the parish, the new rector invited the congregation to evaluate his preaching. He received a barrage of criticism that knocked him for a loop. Fortunately, he had the sense to recognize that he received more criticism than legitimately belonged to him; some belonged to the former rector. He subsequently invited the former rector back and structured an opportunity for parishioners to give him some feedback directly. As it turned out, the former rector had terminated his ministry in a manner that angered and upset many parishioners. Lacking the opportunity to express that hurt and anger directly, they had used the sermon evaluation session to heap criticism on the new rector.

If you encounter anger in your new situation, it's important to evaluate carefully whether it legitimately belongs to you or is meant for your predecessor. Perhaps parishioners are thinking, "If we had treated him properly, he might not have left" or "We really wanted her to leave, but we feel guilty about the way we forced her out."

As with all guilt, forgiveness, and resolution are the key. Depending on the kind of guilt parishioners are expressing, you may be able to invite your predecessor back and, in so doing, gain some healing resolution.

Bargaining is another emotion to watch for. Parishioners may be bargaining with you and the parish to gain your promise that if they retain their memberships, you will be much like your predecessor —or very much unlike her/him.

You may sense bargaining going on when people ask you to do things a certain way. Realize that some parishioners may indeed decide to leave if you choose not to bargain with them the way they desire. Don't take it personally. With every transition, some people

---

Learning to Share the Ministry, by James R. Adams and Celia A. Hahn, Alban Institute, 1975.

leave because the new pastor just doesn't make it for them. If you could please them, you would alienate others, so don't waste energy trying to win at that game. Accept the fact that some people will leave the church within the first year of your ministry and others will move from being very active to being inactive. Still others will join the parish—or will move from being inactive to being active—because of you. In the bargaining game, you should try to be reasonable and open. It is important that you not sacrifice your authenticity by promising what you know you cannot deliver.

Bargaining and losing is one of the tougher parts of start ups. Don't be discouraged. Seek out some active, reliable members and get their perspectives on the matter.

Within the first year of your new pastorate you will have to deal with your own grief, your family's grief, and the grief that remains in the parish. If, with support, you can remain open and pastoral, you will be rewarded with a solid resolution and the sense of acceptance that comes at the end of the grief process. Your parish will then be ready to affirm and install you as their pastor—only this time for real.

CHAPTER IV

Coping with the Stress of Transition

Life Changes

All transitions produce stress. This is true whether you are making a major change in your work, housing, environment, or whether you are simply changing your eating or sleeping habits. Any time we change the way we normally do things, we are adding stress to our lives.

Not all stress, however, should be thought of as negative. Stress can be a very positive factor in our lives. It can be the thing that breaks through our boredom or lethargy and pushes us to our growing edge once again. Without any stress in our lives, we might not get out of bed in the morning.

We should be concerned, then, when our stress level is either too low or too high. Just after moving to a new parish, your stress level most likely will be too high, and high stress levels can diminish your effectiveness as you begin your ministry.

To put you more closely in touch with your stress level, take a minute now to complete the following inventory.

CLERGY STRESS INVENTORY

(Roy M. Oswald, adapted from the stress survey conducted by Dr. Thomas H. Holmes at the University of Washington)

On this page is a list of events in the lives of clergy which have been found to produce individual stress reactions. The scale value of each event reflects the amount of stress and disruption it causes in the life of an average clergyperson. If any of the things mentioned in the survey has happened to you within the last twelve months, record that score in the right-hand column.

Event	Scale Value	Your Score
Death of spouse	100	
Divorce	73	
Marital separation	65	
Death of close family member	63	
Personal injury or illness	53	
Marriage	50	
Serious decline in church attendance	49	
Segment of congregation meeting privately to discuss your resignation	47	
Being forced out of last parish	45	
Marital reconciliation	45	
Retirement	45	
Change in health of family member	44	
Pregnancy	40	
Sex difficulties	39	
Spouse loses important career post	39	
Alienation from one's Board/Council/Session/Vestry	39	
Gain of new family member	39	
Change in financial state	38	
Death of close friend	37	
Increased dissonance with spouse	35	
Merger of two or more congregations	35	
Children in stress	33	
Parish in serious financial straits	32	
Mortgage over $80,000	31	
Difficulty with member of church staff (associates, organist, choir director, secretary, janitor, etc.)	31	
Living with rumors about self/family	30	
Foreclosure of mortgage or loan	30	
Church burns down	30	
Son or daughter leaving home	29	

Event	Scale Value	Your Score
Trouble with in-laws	29	_____
Influential church-member's anger over something you did	29	_____
Slow, steady decline in attendance	29	_____
Outstanding personal achievement	28	_____
Introduction of new hymnal to worship serivce	28	_____
Failure of church to make payroll	27	_____
Remodeling or building program	27	_____
Spouse begins or stops work	26	_____
Begin or end school	26	_____
Death of a peer	26	_____
Receiving a call to another parish	26	_____
Change in living conditions	25	_____
Revision of personal habits	24	_____
Former pastor active in parish in negative way	24	_____
Difficulty with Confirmation Class	22	
Change in residence	20	_____
Change in schools	20	_____
Change in recreation	19	_____
Change in social activities	18	_____
Death/moving away of good leader	18	
Mortgage or loan less than $80,000	17	_____
Change in sleeping habits	16	_____
Change in family reunions/gatherings	15	_____
Change in eating habits	15	_____
Stressful continuing education experience	15	_____
Major program change	15	_____
Vacation	13	_____
Christmas	12	_____
Lent	12	_____
Easter	12	_____
Minor violations of the law	11	_____
Your Total:		_____

If you have just completed a move, you will probably find your score exceeding 200. More than 200 units accumulated during a twelve-month period can cause some individuals to exceed their stress tolerance with resulting physical and/or psychological reactions. Yet each of us has a different threshold level for stress. You may find you are coping quite well in spite of your high score. It's important that you begin to recognize when your threshold level for stress has been reached or surpassed. This inventory also will help you be clearer about the things that add stress to your life.

In completing the survey, were you surprised at the variety of things that contribute to your stress level? For example, were you surprised that such things as an outstanding personal achievement, any changes in your marital relationship, whether positive or negative, changes in personal habits, Christmas and other holidays, and even a vacation are all stress-producing?

Knowing what factors contribute to your stress level will help you know where to look when you wish to decrease your current level of stress.

How will you know when your threshold level of stress is being realized or surpassed?

—Inability to sleep
—Nervousness
—Loss of appetite or eating compulsively
—Inability to concentrate

One other sign might be the experience of having something minor completely wipe you out. Getting a speeding ticket, for example, may not be that bothersome normally. But if you find yourself rendered dysfunctional because of it and need to take the rest of the afternoon off, you may be very near your stress threshold level. Small things can put you over the top very easily.

Several negative things will occur when your threshold level is surpassed:

1. Your perception ability will decrease. You will find yourself unable to listen, watch, or perceive things the way you normally could.
2. You will perceive the options open to you as being greatly decreased. When under normal circumstances you could usually see eight to twelve options open to you in a given situation, now you're able to see only three or four.
3. You will regress to more infantile behavior. You will revert back to old familiar patterns of doing things.

These three results of stress overload will hinder you as you begin a ministry in a new parish. If anything, you will want your perception ability to be at its best during this start-up time. You will want to be able to see as many options as possible. You will not want to regress to more infantile behavior, because such reactive patterns may be self-defeating. So, during your start-up period, you'll need to do some hard work to reduce the amount of stress in your life. You'll want to take hold of those aspects of your life over which you have some control. It's like being out at sea in a sailboat while a storm's brewing. You have no control over the storm that's threatening to invade your life. So you work with the things on your boat which you can control: you take down the sail, batten down the hatches, secure the movable parts, alert the Coast Guard of your whereabouts, and dress for possible rain and wind. For clues to the areas of your life over which you have some control while in a transition period, go back over the stress inventory list. Do you see things that are currently in flux which you can stabilize?

Another way of looking at this is to work with the following diagram:

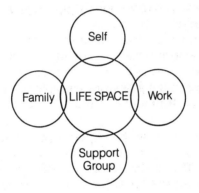

If one or two or three of these outside circles are in flux, is there a way to stabilize the circle over which you have some control?

For example, if you lose your support group in a transition, and your work situation is changing, what can you do to stabilize the areas of life labeled "Self" and "Family"?

The book *Passages* by Gail Sheehy (Dutton, 1972) has given us great insight into what happens to a self in transition. Some of these transitions are out of our control. But we can refrain from:

—Going on a diet
—Changing our eating habits
—Changing our sleeping patterns
—Changing our normal routine of doing things

Similarly we can stabilize the family structure even more during a transition:

—Observing religiously all family rituals and customs
—Spending more rather than less time with the family during the start-up time
—For the sake of family stability, we may consciously plan several trips "back to the old neighborhood" so spouse and kids can be with old friends and in familiar settings again.

Vigilance about your stress level and the stress level of your family should continue for eighteen months after your move. Those who work in crisis intervention situations usually try to give support to individuals for a minimum of eighteen months following a critical incident. People often need to experience the whole cycle of seasons and special events before they begin to sense that life is normal again. The first Christmas in a new situation will seem strange and new. The following year we begin to expect familiar things to happen. When we've done the cycle one-and-a-half times, we *may* settle back and become less anxious.

One other tip for reducing individual stress: for many people physical activity is enormously therapeutic during times of stress. You may think you don't have time, especially during the start-up period, but it is important to maintain your regular pace of physical exercise and activity. If possible, build some time for physical activity into your daily routine.

The Stress Threshold

As mentioned earlier, stress does not really become a significant factor in your transition until your threshold level has been surpassed. The next question is obvious: "How will I know? How do I get a fix on what my threshold level really is?"

Realize that we are not dealing with an exact science. Finding your threshold will not be as straightforward as taking your temperature or having your blood pressure checked. Yet we can become more aware of the messages our bodies are sending us. There's a survey which may help you; but first, let's look at the theory behind it.

Too much stress

THRESHOLD LEVEL

Creative stress

RUSTOUT LEVEL

Too little stress

Notice the bottom category named "rustout." This describes people who have too little stress in their lives and are not being pushed/challenged to full capacity. If you have just experienced a geographical relocation, you're probably not at this level. Your concern should be whether you're surpassing the "threshold level" and placing your health in jeopardy.

Stress management involves managing your life in such a way that you keep the stress in your life creative—that is, maintaining your life somewhere between "rustout" and "threshold." Research on creativity and stress completed at the University of Ontario in London, Ontario, revealed a correlation between stress and creativity—up to a certain point. The more stress people experienced, the more creative they became *until* they reached a critical point. From then on, they became quite un-creative. They obviously had surpassed their threshold level, and all creative processes began to shut down.

We can see readily why beginning a new ministry and functioning beyond one's threshold level of stress would not be a good idea. Not only will one's creativity be shot, but, as stated earlier, one's ability to take in information and to entertain options will be greatly diminished. And, more than likely, one will exhibit some form of infantile behavior—a good way to shoot oneself in the foot in the early months of ministry.

A better alternative is to carefully monitor your stress level and make sure you spend the majority of your time below your stress threshold level. When you know you're above the line, do what needs to be done to get your life and work under better control. In a later section of this book we will explore a variety of self-care coping strategies to help you manage excessive stress.

For now try to get a fix on where you are in relation to your threshold level. The following measurement instrument, although a rough guide, can help you.

THE STRAIN RESPONSE

The Strain Responses Inventory* is another way to measure whether you are living your life below, above, or just at your stress threshold. Stress that is no longer productive for us usually results in some sort of strain on our lives.

Strain Responses Inventory

0 = Never   1 = Infrequently   2 = Frequently   3 = Regularly

_____ 1. Eat too much
_____ 2. Drink too much alcohol
_____ 3. Smoke more than usual
_____ 4. Feel tense, uptight, fidgety
_____ 5. Feel depressed or remorseful
_____ 6. Like myself less
_____ 7. Have difficulty going to sleep or staying asleep
_____ 8. Feel restless and unable to concentrate
_____ 9. Have decreased interest in sex
_____ 10. Have increased interest in sex
_____ 11. Have loss of appetite
_____ 12. Feel tired/low energy
_____ 13. Feel irritable
_____ 14. Think about suicide
_____ 15. Become less communicative
_____ 16. Feel disoriented or overwhelmed
_____ 17. Have difficulty getting up in the morning
_____ 18. Have headaches
_____ 19. Have upset stomach
_____ 20. Have sweaty and/or trembling hands
_____ 21. Have shortness of breath and sighing
_____ 22. Let things slide
_____ 23. Misdirect anger
_____ 24. Feel "unhealthy"
_____ 25. Feel time pressure, anxious about too much to do in too little time
_____ 26. Use prescription drugs to relax
_____ 27. Use medication for high blood pressure
_____ 28. Depend on recreational drugs to relax
_____ 29. Have anxiety about the future
_____ 30. Have back problems
_____ 31. Unable to clear up a cold, running nose, sore throat, cough, infection, etc.

_____ **Total Score**

	0 - 20	Below average strain in your life.
____	21 - 30	Stress starting to show its effects in your life. You are living life near your stress threshold, at times crossing it.
____	31 - 40	Above average strain. Stress is having a very destructive effect on your life. You are living a good portion of your life beyond your stress threshold.
____	Above 40	Unless you do something soon to allieviate your stress, more serious illness will follow.

*Adapted from John D. Adams' survey, "The Strain Response." Used with permission.

Living Life Beyond Your Threshold Level of Stress

For those of you with a strain response score of 25 or more, I want to be clear and direct. This is a simple instrument that reflects the accumulated stress phenomena in your life: eg. sweaty palms, restlessness, feeling depressed, etc. Your body doesn't lie. For the moment, it's telling you that you are pushing too hard. Even so, there's no reason to panic. All of us have lived life beyond our threshold level and have survived. Nevertheless, you should not leave these signs of stress unattended. Your body is whispering, "Slow down. Take better care of yourself." If that whisper is not heeded, it will soon turn into a shout—such as a more serious physical or emotional trauma. Over time stress can be quite deadly; it is the number one killer in North America today. Yet obituaries don't say that someone has died of stress. They simply list some of the key stress-related diseases: HEART ATTACK (1,500,000 people will have a heart attack in the next twelve months and half of them will die within the year); CANCER (800,000 people will contract new forms of cancer in the next twelve months); ALCOHOLISM, DIABETES, AUTO-MOBILE ACCIDENTS. There is a stress factor involved in all of these.

We need to change our perspectives on how disease happens. Normally we assume a "victim mentality" about disease, thinking that some poor sucker was unfortunate enough to have a heart attack or to contract cancer. Instead we need to see more clearly that disease strikes an already unhealthy system. When we are living life beyond our threshold level of stress, our bodies are not in a healthy state.

Being human means in part only being able to tolerate so much flux and change in our lives. Alvin Toffler in his book *Future Shock* (Bantam 1970), explained this to us years ago. All of us need certain amounts of continuity and stability in our lives or we suffer. When too little is familiar and predictable in our lives, we get sick. Sometimes we die.

This is one of the reasons the pastorate is considered a high stress profession. Much of a clergyperson's life is unpredictable and surprising. This is especially true when we accept a call to another parish and must move ourselves and our families geographically.

What are the ways you can simplify your life for the next six months? How can you build more familiarity and predictability into your life right now? Are there family customs, rituals, or traditions that you can return to quickly in your new home? What are the self-care coping strategies which have the best chance of taking hold in your life right now?

Self-Care Coping Strategies

Self-care begins as we learn to differentiate between self-indulgence and being good to oneself. The distinction may seem blurred at times, but the two are very different. Self-indulgence rewards the self for whatever reasons, but in the long run destroys personal health. Self-care responds to the goal of long-term health. I invite you to join me in the struggle to differentiate between the two and to become better at choosing self-care.

It's important to distinguish between narcissism and self-care for the sake of the kingdom. We live in a narcissistic world, and most of us know people who have made their own health the number-one goal in their lives. Self-care *for the sake of the kingdom,* on the other hand, involves strategies for maintaining your health not just for your own sake but for the sake of the people in your congregation. When your body goes, you are a liability to ministry. The church has a cripple on its hands. Similarly, if you engage in self-abusive personal habits, you will be shortening your ministry by years. For example, persons who leave high blood pressure unattended can shorten their lives by as much as 28 years. Ultimately, self-care practices will allow us to serve others better. We are really talking about practicing good stewardship of our bodies and our lives.

A common myth we encounter in our pastorate start up seminars is the notion that we can "bust a gut" in the first twelve months of a new ministry until things are "under control" and then ease back into a more reasonable work schedule. Contrary to expectations, we end up setting in motion work patterns which lead to high levels of stress in the first year and burnout in later years. Rather than being able to back off to a more reasonable work

schedule after the first year, we find ourselves creating expectations
that will require a heavier and a more demanding schedule.

In the early months of a new ministry, it is important to establish work patterns that will not only keep you in good health over
the long haul but will fulfill your parish's major role expectations as
well. If role expectations seem destined to lead to your physical or
emotional breakdown, then some serious negotiations need to take
place.

As a rule of thumb, you should be able to meet your main role
expectations within a 50-55-hour work week. There will be excep-
tions, of course, but stepping over that limit means paying a price.
You'll have little time for rest, exercise or proper nutrition, and
your body will know it. Your family life may suffer from lack of
quality time with your spouse and children. Your spiritual life may
suffer from insufficient time to pray, read, reflect, keep a journal, or
study the Scriptures. You lose and the congregation loses. Astute lay
leaders know this and will press hard for their clergy to refrain
from continually working long hours.

What is needed is good time management so that the parish still
gets five 10-hour days. Think about yourself. What work patterns
keep you in optimum health over the long haul? How do you think
those work patterns match up to the role expectations of your parish? Is there support in the parish for the development of healthy
patterns right from the start of your new ministry?

One potent self-care strategy is coming to terms with human
limitations and beginning to work reasonable hours each week.
Burnout is a disease of the overcommitted. The overcommitted person refuses to listen to his/her body when it whispers. All the great
religious leaders of the past, including Jesus, had to do their ministry within the confines of human limitations. So should you.

Other self-care strategies include those activities and disciplines
which move us toward greater health in any one of the following
three dimensions of life. Take a moment to rate yourself on this
simple scale.

	Poor Health			Optimum Health		
Physical Health	1	2	3	4	5	6
Emotional Health	1	2	3	4	5	6
Spiritual Health	1	2	3	4	5	6

Your rating may help guide you to where you need to develop
some strategies for developing greater health. Holistic health theory
says that improvement in any one of the above categories increases
our health in the other categories as well.

You probably know intuitively what you need to do for yourself to sustain your health during this time of transition. What will it take to put that plan into action? Where is there support for your commitment to that discipline?

Following are some coping strategies which have worked for others:

1. Spiritual formation (Scripture, prayer, worship, meditation, journaling, affirmations, fasting, chanting, retreats, finding a spiritual director, tai chi, etc.)
2. Letting go techniques (bio-feedback,* autogenic training,** meditation, yoga)
3. Support networks
4. Regular vigorous exercise
5. Routes to detachment (woodwork, photography, needlepoint, etc.)
6. Monitoring your intake (food, drink, television, movies)
7. Positive addiction (meditation, running, cycling, swimming)

Which of these have the greatest chance of succeeding in your life right now? Which ones have the capacity to improve your health so significantly that you will be able to raise your threshold level of stress?

---

bio-feedback: With the help of metabolic monitoring devices, individuals can teach themselves how to move to ever deeper states of relaxation. Bio-feedback machines can measure brain waves, blood pressure, skin temperature, pulse rate, etc. The feedback from these machines communicate to the individual when they are doing things that get them to relax. *Bio Dots* are inexpensive, simple Bio-feedback tools.

**autogenic training:* A comprehensive and successful Western deep relaxation technique developed by the German psychiatrist Johannes H. Schultz in 1932. It is a self-hypnosis technique that systematically relaxes all the major muscles of the body.

CHAPTER V

Making Entry

Your Entry/Exit Styles

Remember the last time you attended a party or some other social engagement? Were you aware of your pattern of entering the room, engaging persons, making your presence known, making contributions to the total group dynamics, disengaging from people, and finally exiting? Transition technologists* indicate that each of us has a pattern of engaging and disengaging with people. They say that this pattern is the same regardless of the length or depth of these relationships and that our sequence of behaviors grows out of our history of engaging and disengaging with people.

Sound preposterous?

If they are right, you will make entry into your new parish in exactly the same way you began ministry in your last parish—and in the same manner as you engaged people at the last party you attended. The good news is this: you can become more fully aware of the sequential pattern of behavior responses you typically use to engage with and disengage from individuals and groups. If this sounds like something you would like to understand as you begin work in your new parish, these few simple exercises and some corresponding theory will shed some light on the issue.

First, the theory:

1. Transitions are better characterized by a step process, than by a smooth shape.

---

*Coping with Stress and Transition, Charles Seashore, Ph.D., NTL Institute, Bethel, ME, July 4-9, 1977.

Engagement

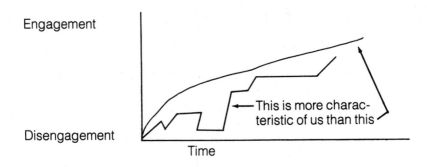

This is more charac-
teristic of us than this

Disengagement

Time

We should be able to identify the points of movement as well as the plateaus. We each have characteristic behaviors on each plateau.

2. Each of us uses a certain pattern of behavior in engaging and disengaging from relationships.

Engagement

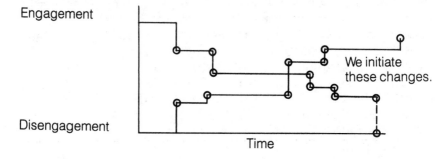

We initiate
these changes.

Disengagement

Time

*Charles Seashore, Ph.D., *Coping with Stress and Transition,* NTL Institute, Bethel, Maine, July 4-9, 1977.

For example, here are some of the things I learned about my own predictable pattern of behavior when entering new groups.

First, in a new setting I will probably remain passive and withdrawn until I've had a chance to psych the place out. I will probably respond enthusiastically to the first person who initiates anything with me in this beginning period, regardless of how attractive or unattractive I find them.

Second, and quite subconsciously, I will look to the women in the group, if there are any, for immediate support. If given an opportunity, I will then take the initiative to become acquainted with several of the women in the room. If by this time I am feeling more confident and affirmed, I will then move to the place where the most excitement is being generated or the most energy is being expended. I will try to make entry into that place or group, and I'll feel good about myself if I'm able to gain acceptance there.

As you can see, I'm somewhat predictable in my entry style. You could chart my movements very specifically on a graph. Similarly, most of us have predictable patterns of disengaging from people or events which can also be charted.

3. It will be easier for us to lengthen or shorten the time we run our entry/exit patterns than to change the pattern itself. It will require something as dramatic as a serious crisis or intensive therapy for us to change our pattern permanently. Through conscious effort, however, we can change it temporarily.

When we forget to be intentional about changing our entry and exiting patterns, we will revert to our old ways.

4. We tend to run our patterns, whether in a twenty-minute encounter on a bus or a twenty-year marriage relationship. As a tadpole recapitulates the history of millions of years of frog development, so I recapitulate my pattern of entering and exiting, regardless of the nature or depth of the relationship.

Now a simple exercise. For this you will need the cooperation of several friends or family members. Have everyone sit around a small table or on the floor. The exercise is done non-verbally, so no talking allowed. Those in the group may represent themselves using their right hands only. All draw imaginary arcs in the air in front of themselves to represent their private spaces. Whenever it suits them, people are to move beyond their private spaces and engage others through the use of their hands. They may touch, explore, hold, push, and grip—whatever comes naturally as they engage others in the center of the table or the floor. When it feels right, they return to their own private spaces.

When everyone is finished, take some time to reflect and share personal perceptions of your own and others' entry and exiting patterns. More than likely everyone will recognize patterns of behavior that are typical of them as they move in and out of groups. The first time I did this exercise I was embarrassed at how my non-verbal behavior typified the way I normally engage with and disengage from individuals and groups.

Reflect on your own style of making entry. For more data, recall your pattern of moving into the last social gathering you attended, especially one where you met some people for the first time.

Once you have identified your usual pattern of making entry, take time to do a careful analysis of your style.

List the various advantages and disadvantages of this typical pattern. What impressions do you usually leave behind? Where are you often open to misinterpretation? What types of people (age, sex, color, creed, size, disposition, etc.) are going to feel affirmed and supported by you and which are not?

Are there things you wish to change about your typical entry-style—especially as you contemplate meeting lots of new people in your new parish? You can alter your style through conscious effort. Remember, however, that you will usually revert to your old familiar pattern when you stop working on making a change.

First Impressions

In the Pastorate Start Up research, we discovered that people place an inordinate amount of emphasis on first impressions. Some people felt that they had a permanent fix on the new minister just by listening and watching him or her at the first service she/he conducted. Others felt that they had the new minister pretty well figured out after a second meeting.

You can't do much about this. The only advice we can give is to be as authentic as you possibly can. The Readiness for Ministry Study of the Association of Theological Schools indicates that lay people value authenticity in clergy more than almost anything else. It helps to remember that people will be anxious about whether their new minister will like them and care about them. They will have difficulties with you if they feel you do not care for them personally. Upon first meeting you, they will be looking for signs and symbols that indicate that you do like them:

    —the way you shake hands
    —the way you listen to them
    —the kind of eye contact they have with you

—non-verbal signals you give that indicate your readiness and openness to engage them personally.

If your new congregation is as heterogeneous as most are these days, it will contain a variety of sub-groups or sub-cultures. The possible range is quite extensive: liberals, moderates, conservatives, high church, low church, young, old, males, females, lesbians and gay men, old guard, newcomers, singles, marrieds, students, city people, country people, charismatics, fundamentalists, etc.

If you can find out in advance which sub-groups are active in this new parish, you will have a distinct advantage. In your first address to the congregation, you may be able to include a few comments, not many, directed at each sub-group. You will be indicating that you are willing to be a pastor to everyone in the congregation, regardless of orientation.

Put yourself in the parishioners' shoes. If you're the house liberal or belong to a small charismatic group that meets in the church, wouldn't you be looking for some sign or symbol—a word—from your new pastor that you are understood and accepted for who you are?

An important ground rule: never go outside your own core set of beliefs in making statements directed at sub-groups. You don't want to promise things you can't deliver later on. This may mean you'll need to think through carefully where you stand with regard to each sub-group. Remember the importance of authenticity. There are probably certain elements of your personality that mesh well with each sub-group. Be in touch with this part of yourself and then express it freely.

Homework

—What are the major sub-groups that make up your new congregation?

—Who are the people that can inform you on this matter?

—Where are the places you can be *genuinely* supportive of each group's particular emphasis?

—How can you include this information in the first few sermons you preach or in some other form of communication within the parish?

Surprises

Our research on pastoral start ups indicates that "surprises" offer one good way of keeping your finger on the pulse during the early months of a new ministry. Surprises are those things that were expected but didn't turn out that way,
OR
the unexpected things that happen, revealing that you had some misperceptions of the church.

In each new relationship, especially as complex a relationship as exists between a pastor and a congregation, gaining insight into the reality of the situation is difficult. Each side brings some fantasies to the relationship. Surprises help us break out of our expectations and anticipations and move closer to reality.

Recording your surprises may reveal a pattern. So try to develop the discipline of writing them down every week. Begin now by noting the surprises that have occurred thus far.

At some point in the opening months of your ministry, ask your official board to reflect for a moment on the surprises they have had about your work with them. If you are candid about what surprises you, they will feel freer to share their own surprises. This is an excellent way to garner feedback from laypeople about your start-up process.

Liking People—The Natural Selection Process

We are convinced that the most important question people have when they first meet their new pastor is: "Will this pastor like me and will this pastor care for me?"

As clergy, we also are anxious about being liked. We may assume that we will be liked for our competence, so we'll put energy into impressing people with our *abilities,* rather than using that energy to communicate to people that we like and care for them.

Place yourself in the shoes of a parishioner who is looking forward to becoming personally acquainted with her/his new pastor. Upon meeting the pastor, she/he gets a subtle, non-verbal message that the new pastor "really doesn't like me." Can you imagine what must go through this parishioner's mind? For the next five to ten years, she or he will have to live with a religious authority that doesn't really care about her or him.

Speed Leas discovered that these kinds of unspoken perceptions can lead to real conflicts in the church. Because lay people find it difficult to say: "We don't think our pastor likes us," they begin to pick on other things that serve a scapegoating function: "He doesn't call," "Her sermons don't make sense," "She can't get anything organized," etc. On the other hand, if there's a love affair between pastor and people, most conflicts can be quickly resolved.

This is why we feel so strongly that clergy new to their congregations should spend six to nine months being little more than a lover and a historian. It's hard work getting to know almost everyone and finding something you can love them for. When all the energy goes into changing the parish around, this outreach will get little attention. The long-term effects can be costly.

It is important also to get in touch with our own natural selection process. We are human. Some people we will find attractive and others will turn us off. We even may find some repulsive. Yet we are called to be a pastor to all people. Both the people who turn us on and the people who turn us off may cause problems for us in the ministry that lies ahead. We will tend to favor those who turn us on and give them attractive assignments. Then we'll have trouble confronting them if they act irresponsibly. Other parishioners will notice how we favor some and may harbor resentment.

Those who turn us off we may avoid unconsciously. We won't think of them when important jobs come up. We will find it difficult to go see them when pastoral crises arise.

Being more clearly in touch with our natural selection process in a start-up period can be quite useful. Try this exercise to help you get in touch with this subjective selection process. Go to a crowded public place where you don't know anybody. Shopping centers are ideal for this exercise. As you come upon people, determine whether or not you are attracted to or interested in them. Make sure the answer is a decisive "yes" or "no." Then try to figure out what it is about them that makes you answer the way you do. Is it because they are male, female, young, old, healthy, unhealthy, smoker, unkempt, long-haired, wearing glasses, or have an odd shape or size? Try to get to the roots of your feelings. Soon you will begin to see a pattern developing.

Knowing what kinds of persons you're naturally drawn to and those you are not will help you handle your first meetings in your new parish more successfully. Remember, you are called to be pastor to all these people, whether you like them or not. Congregation members will be looking for subtle verbal cues or non-verbal expressions. How you respond will determine their first impression of you. These initial interactions are important. Plan well how you manage them.

CHAPTER VI

Taking History Seriously

What kind of information do you need in order to move about with some freedom, knowing you won't violate the more revered norms and standard patterns of behavior in your new parish? To be sure, parishioners will make allowances for the fact that you are new to the place. The question still remains. If you desire to move in with some sensitivity to where people are, how can you be in touch with what is important to know?

In our pastorate start up work, we concluded that the most helpful information of this sort would *not* be found in the material you received when considering the parish. You need to know the parish's sense of its own history. The thing these people consider important—be it a norm, custom, or habit—has some historical event connected to it. People wish to perpetuate a certain way of doing things because they find it one way to recollect their own history.

For this reason, we recommend that you take the history of your new parish seriously. By this we do not mean that you must be stuck with these "ways of doing things" forever. It simply makes sense that in the beginning you respect where people are and what they value. Perhaps later they will participate with you in changing some of the more destructive patterns in their corporate life.

You need not do anything special to be in touch with the oral history of the parish. (Oral, rather than factual, history becomes valuable because what people think happened is more important than what actually did happen.) In your normal routine of being with people, they will want to tell you their version of the parish's history. They will talk about former ministers, key decisions, critical incidents, days of celebration and joy, good times, etc. This is their myth about themselves. Because our myths about ourselves control our behavior, it's important that you be well grounded in this parish's myth. Listen carefully as people put you in touch with this myth.

As you listen, allow your natural curiosity about how they interpret their history to take over. Make some mental notes to yourself and write them down when you are alone. Continue to think about the meaning of this history to these people. Don't be afraid to ask about anything that puzzles you or doesn't seem to fit. Parishioners will be only too happy to share their impressions of the past with you. And they will respect you for taking seriously that part of their corporate life.

If you have already been in the new parish for a number of weeks or months, take a minute now to get out a piece of paper and write down the important historical events of this parish. To help focus your recall, the following peg-hooks may be useful:

1. The congregation's beginnings
2. The leaders or "heroes" that are remembered
3. "Days of Glory" that are recalled
4. Remembrances of crises and turmoil
5. The hopes and dreams that have accumulated over the years, usually associated with the church buildings
6. Families or individuals who were key to this history, some of whom may still be around.

As you work with these items, you may discover:

a. that you know more than you thought you did
b. that there are significant gaps in the information you have.

This may serve to inform you as to what information you need to go after in future encounters with parishioners.

If you desire a more disciplined approach to this historicizing process, we would recommend the following:*

Invite a group of people to spend an evening or Saturday after-

---

*This process was designed by Management Design, Inc., 8250 Winton Road, Cincinnati, OH 45231. It is contained in *Strengthening the Local Church Workbook,* United Church of Christ, 297 Park Avenue South, New York, NY 10010.

noon with you in historical recollection and reflection. Try to contract for three and a half to four hours with them. You may want to
make this a potluck dinner event. If a large group shows up, divide
them into groups of 12 to 15. If there are 25 or fewer, keep them
together in one group. Paste several large sheets of newsprint to
the wall. Draw a line horizontally through the middle of the sheets.
At the far right of the sheets, draw a vertical line and label it "The
Present." In the first hour, invite the group to begin with the present and work backwards into the past, recording on newsprint the
important historical events of the parish that they can remember.
(They should do this without the aid of any written documents.) If
you have more than one group working on this, at the end of the
hour invite them to share what they wrote down. Then have them
combine events to make one single time-line.

During the second hour ask the participants to develop *Meaning Statements* as a way of interpreting the historical events they
have just recorded. Ask the question: "What meaning do these
events, taken together, have for us and our church?"

These meaning statements will give you the interpretation you
need in order to understand the history of this parish better.

One last step: have each person select a meaning statement that
is of particular significance to her/him. Ask the members of the
group(s) to share their investment in the continuity of particular
values/norms/activities. This should help you see where people are
committed to working in the future. It will also inform you as to
their investment in the perpetuation of certain historical perceptions.

Take some time now to reflect on your own history and personal experience within the church. Try to be in touch with the experiences that have made a deep impression on you. The following
questions may aid your reflection:

1. How would you describe your home church(es) to an out-
   sider (or former churches, as the case may be)?
2. What parts of the life of that church had particular meaning?
3. What are the things you valued in the worship service?
4. Who were the heroes of your past in the church (individual
   members, teachers, leaders, ministers, friends)?

      a. Which ones helped to shape your faith and beliefs?

      b. Describe the theology of these heroes.

      c. Describe also their lifestyle and attitudes about church, people, family, money, etc.

5. What are the historical origins of some of the things you value deeply within church life?

Now take your history and compare it with the history of your new parish. As you reflect on the two histories, jot down some notes on areas of compatability and potential tension. For example, try to sense the difference between your heroes of the faith and their heroes of the past.

Your past—indeed, the myths about yourself—has guided and shaped your values, patterns of behavior, and expectations. For example, if you discover from the parish historicizing process that many members value an informal worship experience, while your own history favors a more formal, liturgical service, you will have pinpointed potential tension.

If you have hired a consultant to work through the historicizing process with you, ask the consultant to interview you in front of the group, recording on newsprint the important historical events of your life. Then place your historical time-line alongside the congregation's and invite comments about compatibility and possible areas of difference. Your goal here is mutual understanding.

Having completed this important history-gathering process, you can be more intentional about your ministry in this new place. You can see what elements in the church's history you need to support and nurture. You can begin to assess which factors will contribute to the quality of corporate life and future growth and development.

Taking history seriously will not only make for a good entry but will also aid you in developing a plan of ministry during these early months.

CHAPTER VII

Assessment of Leadership Styles

Assessing leadership styles should take place on two levels:

1. Your typical leadership style
2. The leadership expectations of the parish

The match between these two will greatly influence your effectiveness in this new congregation.

Back in 1958 Robert Tannenbaum and Warren Schmidt conducted a study aimed at discovering a leadership style which would be superior to all others.* Their experiment uncovered a whole new way of looking at leadership. It became clear that *the most effective leadership style was that which matched the leadership expectations (or needs) of the people being led.*

In short, if your new congregation is accustomed to and expects authoritarian leadership, you will be most effective if you can be authoritarian. If they expect laissez-faire leadership, you'll be most effective if you respond that way.

The theory is simple to understand. Applying it becomes more difficult. The following graphic may be helpful in determining both your preference and that of the parish.

Initiative of Pastor

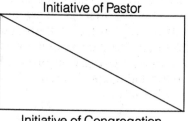

Initiative of Congregation

---

*Robert Tannenbaum and Warren Schmidt, *How to Choose a Leadership Pattern*, Harvard Business Review, March/April 1958.

Where would you place yourself on this continuum? Where would you place your new parish? You can test your hunch in a variety of ways:

1) The most valuable way of assessing the leadership expectation of the new parish is in the historicizing process described in the last chapter. Within the parish's history you'll probably find the congregation's prevailing leadership style preference. This parish ran best—even flourished—under a certain type of pastoral leadership. People who joined the congregation during those times probably valued a certain type of interaction between pastor and people.

2) You can gain information about preferred leadership style by looking at the experience of your immediate predecessor, especially if it was a long pastorate. He/she may or may not have lived up to the leadership expectations of the parish. Ask parishioners with an analytic perspective to measure the effectiveness of your predecessor's leadership style. What more would they have wished for? What would they have preferred less of? What did they most appreciate?

3) A third way to discover leadership expectations is simply observation. At the first meetings you attended did you sense what people were looking for? When did they defer to you? What types of questions were directed to you?

4) You could simply ask your church council what leadership expectations they have for you? Don't be surprised, however, if they are somewhat vague and unclear. More than likely they don't know what they want. What they are able to articulate may be their sense of what *ought to be*. They may talk of wanting to share the ministry, but in reality they want you to take charge.

It is important to understand clearly that you may not be able to live up their leadership expectations entirely—unless you are extremely flexible in your style. Keep in mind that lay people value your authenticity more than a certain leadership style.

We must assume, however, that you have a certain range of leadership styles with which you feel comfortable. The above theory implies that you must move to the extreme of your range in the first years of ministry in a new parish in order to meet the congregation's needs and expectations. A diagram of this process might look something like what follows:

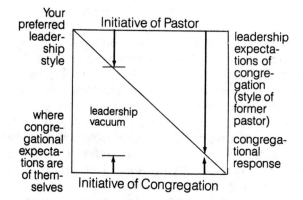

If your parish's leadership expectations are far to the right, you need to move to the right side of your range of leadership styles. When you have gotten as close to the expected leadership style as possible while remaining within what is authentically you, you should be able to negotiate the remaining gap with your lay leaders. You may never be a perfect match to their expectations, but being "close enough" allows for lay leaders to respond, support, and fill in the gaps.

CHAPTER VIII

Making Changes

One of the most controversial issues in our Pastorate Start Up research revolved around clergy initiating changes upon arrival in their new parishes. Although some have done this without a lot of serious repercussions, we believe that making changes upon arrival can cause difficulty.

In the first place, changing things too quickly undermines the ministry of the lay persons and communicates to them that they are doing things all wrong. Second, your changes imply that only professional clergypersons have all the answers. Both effects may undermine your ministry later on.

Therefore, we recommend that new pastors initiate no changes for at least the first six months. Instead, clergy should move about, listening and watching intently what is going on and how people get things done. Clergy should take careful note of those activities and programs which work well, are helpful, and are worth preserving. It is especially important to affirm and support such activities. But don't just affirm and then move on to other things. A young Baptist minister in Kansas arrived in a new parish to find an undershepherd program thriving. So he didn't pay much attention to it until the end of his first year when he found that the program had completely disintegrated! More than likely, the lay people perceived from the pastor's inattention that he didn't think the program was important. So they withdrew their energies from it.

Take a minute now to reflect on those programs and activities in your new parish that are much too important to be dropped. Don't take anything for granted. Include the choir and the Sunday School in this evaluation.

Now, look at your list and think about ways you will communicate your affirmation and support of these programs.

Let's switch attention now to the first major change you will make in the parish. It is worth some special thought as it will gain the attention of the entire congregation. What is more, when you begin to solicit lay persons to help in initiating this new emphasis or program, you will probably receive wide support for it.

We have discovered that transitional periods give rise to a good deal of energy and excitement. People expect new and invigorating things to happen. They also wish to affirm their new minister. Hence, they will say "yes" to her/his *first* request.

That's why your choice for the first big change is so important. Your first change will probably succeed with flying colors, but your second and third changes may come with more difficulty. One of the mistakes clergy make most frequently is using up this initial energy on one of their favorite programs or customs. Instead some serious thought should go into the best change to make first. To help you in your discovery, ask yourself these questions:

—Where is this parish in difficulty?
—What are the things that will block this parish from having a
   viable future?

Your first major change effort should be in response to those areas of greatest need. You'll probably regret it if you use up new energy on your favorite issue, when you could have gotten the parish on a much firmer footing. Here are some other questions to consider:

—Are there destructive norms existing in the parish? What are
   they?
—Does the parish have a solid financial base?
—Are people's needs being met by what the parish currently
   offers?
—Is the parish living up to its leadership potential?
—Is a good percentage of the parish involved in weekly
   worship?

Your first major change should grow out of answers to these questions. Take some time now to engage in that kind of deeper analysis of the parish. When you have chosen the top two or three things the parish needs in order to have a viable future, check out your analysis with several key lay people. If they concur with your analysis, take it to your Board/Council/Session/Vestry.

To summarize, make no changes in the first six to nine months of your new ministry. Your task during this period is to be a lover and a historian. Your first change effort should be a significant one, forming the foundation upon which the future health and vitality of the parish will rest. By holding off on the first major change you give yourself the opportunity to grasp the power dynamics of the parish.

CHAPTER IX

Gaining Role Clarity

A good deal of evidence supports the notion that calling a pastor fulfills a role rather than a job description. That is, if you added up all the specific tasks a pastor normally performs, that would not adequately define the pastor's role. Included in role definition are all the projections and expectations of the people to be served. That's why writing job descriptions for clergy and then engaging them in performance appraisals often ends up being unproductive. Such an exercise does not get at the essence of what it means to be pastor.

Instead of a job description, clergy and their parishes need role clarification. It is extremely important for a pastor to be clear about the expectations a congregation has of her/him. Implicit in role clarification is some understanding of the purpose of the parish. What does it mean to be a Grace Lutheran Church in Washington, D.C., and what is the role of the pastor in helping the congregation fulfill its purpose? Behind the question of purpose are assumptions around how a parish relates to society. How does the role of the pastor incorporate those assumptions?

Gaining role clarity requires hard work over a long period. In fact, clergy probably need to work at role clarity throughout their ministries. In general, the laity is genuinely confused about what the role of a pastor should contain. Each lay person has a different expectation of her/his pastor.

Issues around role identity help explain why the pastorate is such a high stress occupation. Clergy malaise concerning their role can take at least three forms:

1. Role ambiguity—being unclear as to what expectations one's role contains.
2. Role confusion—members holding different, often contradicatory, role expectations of a clergyperson.

3. Role overload—clergy becoming overwhelmed by all the expectations coming in at them.

Although role clarity may take years to achieve, the work of clarification needs to begin early—that is, in the start-up period. A good place to begin is gaining clarity about one's own role expectation. Once you know what *you* expect from your role, you then can negotiate with individuals and groups within the parish. Sharing expectations is a good way to begin.

In this, the historical reflection process discussed in Chapter 6 can be helpful. Expectations of you as pastor will be similar to the congregation's past experiences with clergy—both their negative and positive experiences. Whether we like it or not, we inherit the credit and debit parishioner's have built up based on their past experiences. This fact should make you curious. For example, if clergy have lied to them in the past, they will watch you very closely in the beginning to see how honest you are with them.

Role negotiation involves dealing as openly as possible with the differences between your own images of pastoring and their expectations. This task would be far easier if the entire congregation held similar perceptions. Don't expect that. You will need to negotiate one role with the congregation as a whole, and then a series of roles with individual parishioners, each of whom is consciously or unconsciously projecting his/her role expectations onto you.

For now, you should try to pull together the variety of messages you have been given in ever so many subtle ways. Do you know which ones you can respond to with integrity and which ones will require some active re-negotiation?

We will explore this subject further in the next chapter.

CHAPTER X

The Psychological Contract

In his book *To Come Alive,** Jim Anderson developed the concept of the psychological contract that exists between each member and his/her congregation. This contract enables members to continue to be involved in the parish because they are getting something they want from their membership.

These psychological contracts cover a broad range. At one end of the continuum are those people who only show up at church at Christmas and Easter and want the miniser to bury them when they die. They don't want a whole lot more from the parish. At the other end of the continuum are those people who not only show up every Sunday for worship, but attend one or two parish meetings a week. They may want a lot of the minister's time and attention. It would be folly for a pastor to deal with people at these two extremes in the same way. For many parishioners the crunch comes when they perceive that the contract is broken and they are no longer getting what they want.

In actual fact, we should probably be talking about two psychological contracts—one parishioners have with the parish and another with the pastor. You should be concerned first with the contract being formed between parishioners and yourself during the early months of your ministry. This often unspoken contract was what I was referring to when I wrote in the last chapter about negotiating your role one-to-one with each parishioner. If you listen carefully, you will notice that you are constantly receiving messages from parishioners as to the kind of pastor they want you to be for them. It is important that you be aware of the negotiating that is already taking place. How you handle the contract will make a big difference in your relationships with parishioners. (This is another

---

**To Come Alive,* Jim Anderson, Harper & Row, NY, 1973.

reason for spending the first six or nine months getting to know people, rather than setting goals or setting up programs.)

Let's look at what happens when a parishioner perceives that you are not delivering on what she/he thought the contract entailed. You visit a shut-in and she/he talks about how a former pastor dropped by to visit once a week. Even though this may be told anecdotally, the subtle request is that you do the same. You may reply that it has been your pactice in the past to visit shut-ins once a quarter. You are actually asking if the shut-in will hang in there with you if you only visit infrequently. Another shut-in may not care if she/he gets a visit from the pastor. Visiting him/her even once a quarter may break the psychological contract.

The messages to clergy are many and varied:

"Please hug me when you see me in church."
"Check in with me after I chair a committee meeting."
"Remember some of my favorite hymns."
"Show up some Friday evening when I'm playing basketball."
"Be there for me when things go crazy with my parents."
"I like an occasional business lunch with my pastor."
"Wear your collar when in church."
"Be affectionate with your wife."

Ministry is not a rational enterprise. In fact, it may seem totally irrational at times. When people must deal with such realities as fear, death, chaos, mystery, and God, they look for a religious authority who will help them cope. Their expectations regarding *how* they want a pastor to help them vary greatly from person to person. Thus the variety of psychological contracts.

A study by the Grubb Institute in London claims that the toughest part of the ordained ministry is coming to terms with role issues. The study suggests that the best preparation for the ministry would be three years of role negotiations. Role issues cannot be learned in a seminary classroom; the only way to come to terms with the role of religious authority in a given community is to actually be in the role.

So begin sensing the role projections coming your way and then learn about the appropriate responses. Begin to learn the difference between "relatedness" and "relationship." You're really dealing with people's expectations of you most of the time. Anyone who doesn't want to deal with the craziness of role projections probably doesn't belong in the ministry.

I encourage you to be somewhat disciplined in your negotiations of psychological contracts with individuals. As you move about the parish interacting with people, take some time following each significant encounter to write down on a three-by-five card:

1. What kind of psychological contract exists between this person and the parish
2. What kind of psychological contract this person wants with you, the pastor.

At first you may find it difficult to be this discerning; you may not be accustomed to thinking in such terms. You don't know how to ask the right questions. But the discipline of note-keeping will encourage you to become more aware of the role negotiation going on all the time, even your own subconscious negotiations.

Be sure to remember some things you wanted for yourself when you worked through the section on Self–care in Chapter 4. You may have good intentions, yet you are subconsciously negotiating away 60 to 70 hours per week. You need not capitulate in this way as long as you let people know clearly that you care about them. As in all bargaining, you and your parish may be in a stand-off for a while to test where there's give-and-take in your relatedness.

If you are new at this game, it is always good to have a mentor with whom to work. You need to watch an old pro deal with projections and transferences. Find one you can consult with occasionally.

CHAPTER XI

Parish Analysis

A Look at Separate Functions

More than likely, you will want to get a fix on your new parish as
soon as possible. Following are some methods that might help you
in this analysis. Each one is like a special set of glasses you put on
to view the parish. We hope this analysis will serve to instruct you
towards a more intentional ministry down the line.

Decision-Making   How are decisions made in this parish? What is
the quality of these decisions? Do they represent the wishes of a
broad base within the congregation or merely that of a select few?
What channels do members have for influencing the decision-making process? Where do you fit into this process?

Communication   How do people find out what is happening
within the parish? Are certain groups more informed than others?
How effective are:

   a. the formal communication efforts within the parish (e.g.,
      newsletters, announcements, letters, etc.)
   b. the informal communication network (how word spreads
      throughout the parish). Are people left out of the informal
      network? How easy is it for people to make something
      known within the parish?

Conflict   What norms within the parish govern how people handle
differences and disagreement? How are differences settled between
groups and between individuals? What do parishioners expect of
the pastor when conflict arises? What has been this parish's history
in dealing with stress or differences?

Creativity How open is the parish to new ideas? How hard do people have to fight to get a new idea heard? What channels do they need to go through? When was the last time a really good idea got implemented in the parish?

Humor Where is it appropriate? What type is enjoyed? Do people need more opportunities to laugh with each other? What are the occasions at which people really let go?

Worship How are the variety of worship needs handled in this parish? Which groups or individuals have their needs met least often? Who decides on the type, style, frequency, and time of worship opportunities?

Piety and Beliefs Some church leaders think that the greatest difference between Christians is not so much differences in theology, but differences in forms of expressing piety. How does the parish prefer to express its devotion to God? What are the belief systems behind these forms of piety?

Human Community Ignore the reason why people are in the church building for the moment. Watch how they interact with one another. What kind of human community is this parish? Are people affirmed and supported? Do members like and enjoy each other? Are there certain kinds of persons who are less welcome in this community (e.g., old, young, handicapped, less intelligent, certain economic backgrounds, homosexuals, blacks, Hispanics, Indians, ex-convicts, singles, divorced persons, etc.)? What would be needed for this to be a more caring, supportive community for the membership?

Power Analysis of a Congregation

Clergy and laity often talk about the formal and informal power structures in a parish. Sometimes major decisions get made by a handful of people, some of whom are not even in official elected positions.

As a person new to the parish, you may speculate as to who these power people are or some of the laity will no doubt inform you. It's important that you discover who holds the formal or informal power in the parish, especially if the way decisions are made confuses or dumbfounds you. Less than comprehensible decision-making patterns usually indicates that those in decision-making positions are checking with other people on the sidelines.

The following exercise will help you analyze parish power networks in a more disciplined way:

Take a single sheet of paper and draw a line down the center lengthwise. Label the sections as follows:

Reputational Power	Official Power
Coalition Power	
Communicational Power	

Under Official Power list all those persons who hold elected offices in the parish. For a large parish, limit this list to those in official decision-making positions.

Under Reputational Power, list that handful of people in the parish who have the respect of most persons in the community. These people have a certain charisma about them. When tough decisions get made in the parish, people usually look sideways to see where these people stand on the issues.

Under Coalition Power, first list all the formal and informal subgroups that exist in the parish. This should include every group

from the choir to the church bowling league. Include also the informal groups that cluster together on Sunday mornings. Also list the
key individuals within each of these sub-groups—those one or two
individuals who are ring-leaders. Depending on how the ringlead-
ers feel about you or an issue, these sub-groups can be mobilized
either for or against you.

Under Communicational Power, list the informal communications networks within the parish. Try to answer the question, "Who
has whose ear?" Who calls whom when there is some news to
share? Include here people who spend a lot of time around the
church building (e.g., church secretary, janitors, retired workers,
etc.). These people usually have a lot of information about the activities of the parish. Accurate information is an important power com-
modity. Those people who know "what's going on" are far more
powerful than those who are in the dark. In this column, list those
people who always seem to be in the know.

You now have people listed under four categories who represent power currencies within a parish. Go over all four lists and
note the names that appear on more than one list. Those names
that appear on two or more lists are the most powerful people in
the parish.

Write these power people's names on a special list. Spend a few
minutes with each name and rate your credibility with each person:

1	2	3	4	5	6
Low					High
Credibility					Credibility

This rating may give you some idea where you need to do some
work if certain issues are to be resolved. You may decide you need
to spend some time with certain folks in order to build a power
base for yourself within the parish.

You also may want to rate each of these people with regard to
their positions on specific issues. For example, if you are up against
a key vote at a congregational meeting, rate each person's views on
that issue:

1	2	3	4	5	6
Negative					Highly
					Supportive

If the majority of these key persons are for the proposal, you
can be fairly sure it will pass. To make sure, you may decide to visit
a few key leaders who seem to be sitting on the fence. We do not

recommend taking an issue to the parish as a whole unless you are fairly certain it will pass. When key issues fail to pass, your credibility and reputation may be diminished. This makes you less powerful when other issues arise.

Two other pieces of analysis also may be helpful. Take a closer look at the coalitions and key leaders you listed under Coalition Power. Then ask yourself the following questions:

—What is the specific self-interest of this group? What values do they espouse? On what issues within the congregation do they become active?

—How unified is this group? Is it likely that the group would split at certain points? Under what circumstances would this happen?

—Where are you with this group? Whose ear do you have in this group? Are there ways you can feed information to it as well as remaining informed about the group's thinking/feeling activity? In short, do you have input rights to the group and also does the group keep you informed of its activities? To increase your influence with the group, where would you begin? With which individuals?

You may be able to follow the same process in evaluating the informal communications systems within the parish. With some work, you may be able to use these systems to great advantage in the parish—or, if that is not possible, at least minimize the damage they can do within the congregation. Begin by looking at what kind of entre you have with each informal communications system. Continue by rating your credibility with the individuals and groups involved.

Power dynamics affect each local parish. Most congregational members have their own assessment of power and control issues within their parishes. This is a given. So deciding whether or not you will undertake a power analysis of the parish is not the issue. At issue is whether you will be good at the process and disciplined in your approach or ignore the issues and handle power poorly. You may have to confront your personal feelings of comfort or discomfort with the use of power and clarify your theology of power.

The Provolutionary Grid

The following framework for analyzing a congregation originated with Dr. Robert Hoover, former chairperson for community planning at the University of Cincinnati.* The theory provides an invaluable tool in assessing where a congregation is in its normal life cycle. The life, death, and resurrection progression describes all of life. Every person and organization comes into existence and develops. Yet every development implies eventual decline—and also the potential for continual renewal and transformation. The graphic below illustrates the concept.

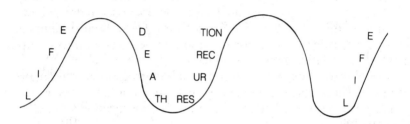

The Provolutionary Grid can be diagrammed in a similar fashion.

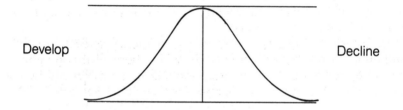

"Provolutionary" means "to turn ahead"—to turn to the future. The provolutionary approach, while dealing with present change, conserves and utilizes energy and creativity by focusing on the development of future possibilities for change (achievement of hopes, dreams, and goals).

The left side of the grid represents the birth and development stages in the life of the organization. The right side represents the process of decline and deterioration. Now let's look in more detail at each side of the grid and the implications for the church.

---

*It was developed by Management Design, IN, 8250 Winton Road, Cincinnati, OH 45231, and produced for the United Church of Christ's Strengthening the Local Church Project. For more details on this grid, as well as other helpful designs for local congregations, we recommend writing for the resource booklet titled *Strengthening the Local Church;* it is available from Office of Church Life and Leadership, United Church of Christ, 297 Park Avenue South, New York, NY 10010.

Provolutionary: Myth-Belief-Norm

To view the developmental side of congregational life we need to look at each parish's "myths," "beliefs," and "norms." The basic assumptions and values at the heart of a congregation's life constitute its myth. Myth here describes a congregation's basic sense of identity. A congregation's myths are created and molded by all its experiences and are passed on from generation to generation through the process of re-telling its history as well as through its ongoing experience. Congregational myths may be unconscious or pre-rational; hence, they may only exist on a feeling level. Some examples of myth are the feeling or assumption that persons are more important or that order is better than chaos.

Myths usually express themselves in congregational statements of belief. Theological formulations, statements of faith, creeds, stated goals, and purposes all help to illumine a congregation's beliefs about itself.

Norms usually grow directly out of beliefs. A congregation's programs, its structure and relationship, policies and traditions, use of the budget, and treatment of members constitute its norms. Worship services on Sunday mornings, pastoral visits to the sick, all-male governing boards, and filling up the rear pews first are *norms* typical of some local churches.

In a healthy congregation there is consistency and integrity among its myths, beliefs, and norms. When there is discontinuity between these three, the congregation will be characterized by confusion, lack of commitment, apathy, conflict, and decline.

NORMS
_____

to actions and behaviors which express its identity and purpose.

BELIEF
_____

to an articulation of that sense into statements of what it is for

MYTHS
_____

A healthy congregation moves from a sense of who it is

For a congregation to maintain health and vitality it must touch base, again and again, with its myth—to reformulate its statements of belief, purposes, and goals and to engage in new actions and behaviors. The left side of the provolutionary grid can now be described as follows:

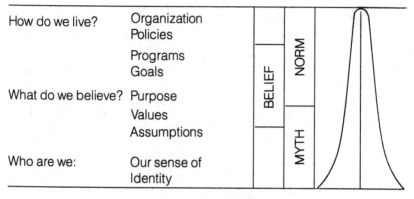

How do we live?	Organization Policies Programs Goals	BELIEF	NORM	
What do we believe?	Purpose Values Assumptions		MYTH	
Who are we:	Our sense of Identity			

Our Sense of Self

As pastor in a new parish, you should check the congruency between the congregation's myths, beliefs, and norms. Does the parish's understanding of itself jibe with its stated beliefs, its values,
and goals? Do these jibe with its policies, programs, and structures?
Take some time now to reflect on this aspect of your new parish.
You may need to talk to some people or engage a small group to
help in this analysis.

You also should look for symptoms of death or decline within
your new congregation. These are typified by stages of descent on
the right side of the provolutionary grid. As no organization is un-
changing, it can be growing and developing in some areas and de-
clining and dying in others. What succeeded with flying colors last
year may lose ground this year.

The three corresponding stages on the right side of the grid are:

"Anomie"—a state of being where organizational norms are
weak or being questioned or challenged

"Ideology"—a state of being where belief statements no longer
are expressive of the commitment and conviction of the
members

"Alienation"—a state in which members no longer share common values and assumptions about the organization, thus are
separated from it both emotionally and intellectually.

One indicator of the health of a congregation is the level of trust that exists within it. Thus an indicator of the sickness of an organization is the lack of trust or level of doubt that prevails.

Five levels of doubt can be identified and illustrated on the right side of the grid:

1. *No Doubt* Myths, beliefs, and norms are all lined up and functioning smoothly and effectively. Enthusiasm and commitment are high. There is maximum acceptance and approval of the congregation's purposes and performance.
2. *Operational Doubt* "How are we doing it?" is a question that characterizes this level of doubt. Operational norms are being called into question (e.g., "Is Sunday Church School the best way to do Christian Education?")
3. *Ideological Doubt* When norm questions are not dealt with, members' questions become more serious and their doubts deepen. They begin to ask questions about the purposes and goals of the parish. Ideology indicates that the only basis for continuing to do what is being done is that "it's the way we have always done it." In other words, the conviction of belief no longer undergirds the practice.
4. *Ethical Doubt* If a congregation remains unresponsive to these concerns, they will intensify. People begin to feel that not only are some programs of the parish not helping folks, they are actually harming them. When people reach this point, they are said to be expressing ethical doubt. The way the organization trusts persons is the key issue.
5. *Absolute Doubt* If the congregation turns a deaf ear to these serious charges, members will either give up and leave, or try to subvert the parish in a variety of ways (e.g., withhold support or organize for resistance or disruption).

These levels of doubt are found on the right side of the provolutionary grid in the following way:

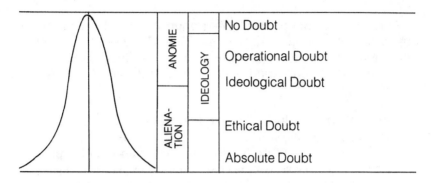

To understand the grid one must see the relationship between the right and left sides. If you can clearly identify which kind of doubt exists in your new parish, you can look on the left side for an appropriate response. For example, when a congregation is in a state of "Anomie"—the absence of commitment to values, programs and actions—the leadership of the parish can creatively respond by moving back to its statement of purpose and its goals to build programs and structures more appropriate to the new situation. Or more specifically, when discontent arises with Church School, the church can move back to its goal of Christian Education and explore other alternatives for addressing this need. This is possible if the members are committed to the goals rather than to the programs.

The level of doubt in your new parish may be deeper and call for another kind of response in order to move it back to life and health. For example, a congregation may rely on old cliches and rationalizations which no longer motivate. A parish may sponsor an annual bazaar to raise money to pay off the building debt and then may be tempted to continue that practice after the debt has been retired. Advocates for the bazaar may talk about its purpose as meeting fellowship needs and providing an opportunity for persons with this interest and talent to serve. The problem is with ideology, in the middle of the right side of the grid. Clues for dealing with it can be found by looking near the middle of the left side: you'll probably want to get back to the church's beliefs (purposes and goals). You might decide to formulate new goals for the bazaar which are consistent with the goals of the church—or more appropriately, you might take the goals being used as ideological support for the bazaar (fellowship, service) and look for new programs to meet those goals.

As you go through this analysis of the congregation, you may discover that at its heart members are alienated from one another and from the organization because of fundamental differences about its values. This is the level of ethical or absolute doubt where the organization can only be maintained if it can connect with its myth again.

The above illustrations are intended to show the relationship between:

—Norm and Anomie
—Belief and Ideology
—Myth and Alienation

Determining how serious are the declines in an organization gives its leadership some clues about where to begin. If an organization is experiencing serious alienation, any attempt to modify things at the norm level by making changes in program and structure will be perceived as inappropriate.

Now we can visualize all that's been said about the dynamics of organizational life on the following provolutionary grid:

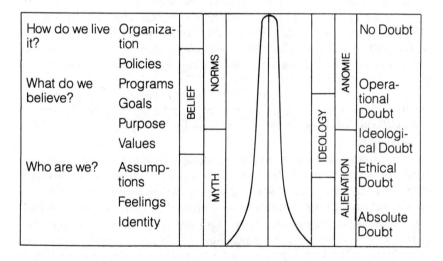

Take some time now to reflect on the kinds of doubt you have been experiencing so far in your new parish. How widespread is this doubt? Using the above theory of organizational life and death, try to determine where your parish is in the cycle. Next, develop appropriate strategies drawn from the left side of the grid which are congruent with the kind of basic work the parish needs to do.

CHAPTER XII

Developing a Plan of Ministry

Our Pastorate Start Up research indicated that a pastor does best to enter a new situation with *no plan* of ministry already prepared. This applies especially to plans for new programs in the parish. The wise pastor moves in willing first to listen and to learn.

While affirming this approach, we see areas where a plan of ministry can be quite appropriate—in particular plans which include better self-care, the avoidance of self-defeating behavior, and the intention of gaining quality feedback from your new congregation. We will look at this kind of planning in this chapter.

Strengths and Self-Defeating Behavior

In your new parish you'd like to use your strengths to the upmost while avoiding those self-defeating patterns of behavior that got you into difficulty in the past. First, we need to make a distinction between weakness and self-defeating patterns. Your weakness may not be detrimental to your service in the ministry. Some clergy are able to utilize weakness to great advantage. A self-defeating behavior, on the other hand, does no one any good. For example, you may have a pattern of continually avoiding conflict. Or you may "fly off the handle" when under pressure. Such self-defeating patterns diminish you and your ministry in the eyes of your parishioners.

For the most part, clergy do not have the opportunity for disciplined reflection on their past ministry before starting a new one. At best some are able to take a bit of vacation time between parishes.

You'll do yourself and your new congregation a favor by taking time now to reflect on the past. Use the diagram provided to chart out your recollections.

Take a sheet of paper and divide it into two columns:

	SELF-DEFEATING PATTERNS OF BEHAVIOR
STRENGTHS	

The following questions may stimulate your memory in each category:

Strengths:

—What are the things I do well and enjoy doing?
—What are the things I do well but don't enjoy doing?
—What are the things that I don't do well but enjoy doing?
—Where are the places where my ministry has been appreciated in the past?
—What have been some of my under-used talents for ministry?
—What are the aspects of ministry for which I have high energy?

Self-Defeating Patterns of Behavior:

—Where in the past have I found myself backed into the same old corners?
—What situations continually de-energize me?
—Under what conditions do I usually tighten up and become defensive?
—What things do I usually put off or postpone which get me in trouble over the long run?
—What types of people (age, sex, physical characteristics, attitudes, behaviors, etc.) do I have the most difficulty with?

—Where do I feel inadequate, unskilled, or under-trained?
—What are the times and places that evoke my anger?

Listing these items is half the battle. Take a minute now to look
back over the list. Star the three most important items for attention.
They were:

_____

_____

_____

It's unlikely you will be able to lead with your strengths consis-
tently or avoid self-defeating patterns of behavior just by listing
items on a sheet of paper. It takes more than an act of will to accomplish this.

The second half of your task is developing a plan whereby you
ensure that your strengths are utilized and your bad behavior patterns are avoided. You need to build in the kind of support, training and evaluation that will help make this happen. In so doing you
will be enhancing yourself as a professional in ministry. You may
even want to consider this as part of your professional development
for the first year.

Some clergy continually find themselves doing work in an area
they know they're weak in. They do this because they are trying to
live up to the expectations of others. What do you need to do in order to use your major strengths? What will enable your parish to
use your major strengths?

—Who are the people with whom you need to talk for support
  in this venture?
—What decision-making group do you need to negotiate with in
  order to gain support for your areas of strength?
—Who are the other people who need to be convinced that the
  parish will be the winner if you are allowed to go with your
  strengths?

Now let's consider what kind of support you need to deal with
self-defeating patterns of behavior. Is it possible to form a small
group of two or three to help you avoid the kinds of situations we
have been talking about? This group could be made up of either
peers or of trusted parishioners. They should be people who have
the skills and disposition to provide real help.

How can they monitor your behavior and give you feedback on
what they see?

If situations or circumstances need to be avoided, what preliminary steps need to be taken to ensure this?

Would some specialized training be helpful? What are the chances of building this activity into your continuing education for this year?

Would some short-term therapy be helpful? Where can you locate a qualified person whom you like and trust?

Generally, we find two self-defeating patterns most common to clergy:

1. *Passivity* or in some cases passive-aggressive behavior. Introverted-type clergy can often become passive in the face of a leadership vacuum. In the long run passivity gets clergy in more trouble than anything else.
2. *Conflict avoidance* is the other major self-defeating pattern. Feeling types often dislike conflict intensely and avoid it whenever they can. The long-term results are unresolved differences that hang on in the parish. Sometimes conflict-avoiders will move to another parish simply to get away from all the unresolved tensions. We firmly believe that clergy set the tone for how conflict is managed in a parish. When clergy will not confront parish tensions, laity will not want to deal with them either.

If either of these patterns is part of your history, how or why is it persisting? Take some time to write out a plan for confronting such patterns and building a system of support.

Taking Better Care of Yourself

Earlier we looked at how to measure your threshold of stress in a time of transition and how to develop coping strategies. We return to the subject of self care in the context of a plan for ministry. Surviving as a professional within a parish setting is not easy. Living into all the parish expectations detracts from one's own personal/ spiritual development and family life. When clergy allow themselves to become burned out, they join the ranks of thousands who are dead spiritually and crippled emotionally, whose family relationships have a hollow ring to them, and whose physical health is dangerously abused. It is a sorry sight to see young women and men enter the ministry with vigor and enthusiasm only to end up years later as shallow, uninviting people. This happens most often when clergy enter a new situation without an intentional plan of self-care.

Most of us left seminary without much insight into our special needs. It was like being sent out to study plant life in the jungle without being given any survival tools. Whatever survival tactics we had, we developed on our own.

A plan for how you will take better care of yourself in this new setting will allow you to build some givens into your daily life right from the beginning. Now is the time to make such a plan. Later on, when role, norms, and patterns are established, you will find it much more difficult to accomplish this goal.

I invite you to look at three dimensions of your life within the parish using this diagram:

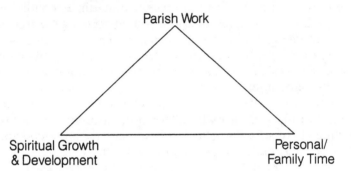

All three areas are important in the life of an effective clergyperson. When one of the three receives little or no attention, one's entire ministry is diminished.

Parish Work involves responding to all the demands for personalized service while pressing for excellence in the programs of parish life. As Jim Glasse says in his book *Putting It Together in The Parish,** you need to pay the rent or very soon your ministry will be in trouble. Beyond paying the rent, most clergy find a whole host of things they must do to protect themselves politically. This entails keeping the parish somewhat off balance as it moves, or is pushed, towards its growing edge, rather than getting bogged down in pettiness, resistance, and hostility.

Personal/Family Time. We dealt with this area earlier, but we

---

Putting It Together in the Parish, James D. Glasse, Abingdon Press, Nashville, TN and New York, NY, 1972.

should take another look at how it relates to our triangle. Married clergy must spend large chunks of time with a spouse and family or the quality of those relationships will diminish. More important than quantity of time is the quality of time spent together. Clergy may be physically present in the home but too exhausted or distracted to make real contact.

Beyond time with one's family, clergy need time for rest, relaxation, and recreation. Because the parish ministry is a rather sedentary profession which involves strong emotional pressures, other more active and healthful outlets are vital.

Spiritual growth and development takes discipline. The person who is ordained to the parish ministry is expected to be a spiritual giant and an expert on all spiritual matters. Yet more than likely, she/he entered seminary as part of a spiritual quest or journey. He/she was looking for some answers to life's deepest questions. At seminary he/she was supposed to develop spiritually by studying Bible, theology, and church history. In reality, any spiritual maturity she/he gained probably happened between academic courses and chapel attendance. The final illusion was that parish work would continue that process of spiritual development.

Instead parish work often drains one spiritually. At this point, we realize that we have not been given all the training and skills needed to take even the first steps on our spiritual journey.

Spiritual maturity usually comes about as a result of some disciplined work in the field. Parishioners expect sermons to have spiritual depth to them, yet few agree to have their pastor spend significant time in personal reflection, prayer, Bible reading, and meditation. They assume that their pastor has done this kind of inner work already.

Clergy generally find it difficult to find time for their own personal/spiritual development. Perhaps they themselves think it would be selfish to spend time in this area. "That's not what I am paid to do," they may think. Yet, in reality, a strong argument could be made that a clergyperson's spiritual life should be her/his first job responsibility.

Let us look again at our triangle. If the space within the triangle represents all the time available to you, you can quickly visualize the tension points in parish ministry. (The curved lines represent time being eaten up.)

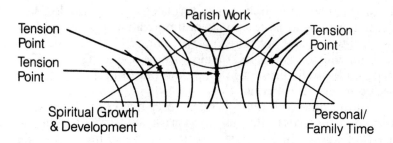

Most clergy are aware of the tension between parish work and personal/family time. Fewer clergy are cognizant of the tension between parish work and spiritual work or between spiritual work and personal time.

We contend that all three areas need time and energy if the ministry is to be holistic and effective over time.

What plans do you have for ensuring quality time in each of these areas? Take a few moments now to shape the kind of time-schedule you intend to keep in this new parish. Begin with your plans for a typical week. What kind of work patterns do you intend to establish which will enable you to take care of necessary work in the parish yet allow time for yourself and your own development, as well as quality rest, relaxation, and recreation with significant others?

Do a time-line of your first year in this parish. Include in the design your plans for:

—a vacation
—longer, non-vacation time with family
—continuing education
—extended periods of time for personal spiritual reflection and development (several Protestant clergy I know spend several days each year in a monastic setting to give themselves large chunks of time for meditation, reflection, and silence.)

The last task in this exercise is the most difficult. More than likely you have scheduled some new time space for yourself that includes things you feel are important to you. So that you don't add that time on top of an already full schedule, you must determine what you will stop doing.

Begin by making a list of the things which you are going to drop from your schedule. Once this list is before you, start developing some plans for making them stick. Whose consent do you need in order to drop items from your schedule? Where and when can you expect to feel some repercussions? What kind of support do you need in order to follow through on these intentions?

Unless you develop this list with specific plans for follow through, your other plans for taking better care of yourself may be for naught. A necessary survival skill in any parish is learning to say "no" to people and being able disengage yourself from time to time. Without this skill you will continually find yourself living into other people's expectations of you. Your life will constantly feel beyond your control.

In our society we need persons who are able to cut through all the madness of frantic activity. These people can possibly serve as models for others. Where else can we expect this but from the church? Clergy can serve quite appropriately as models in this regard.

The three foci of work, self/family, and spiritual formation are important for lay persons as well. They also need to examine how their lives are weighted disproportionately in one arena or another. By taking seriously your use of time, you can invite others to do the same. You may even encourage some lay persons to join you in taking time out for spiritual development.

Developing Support Systems for Yourself

In several sections of this book we talk about developing a good support system for yourself so that you can move well into termination, transition, and start up. Now it's time to look at what constitutes a good support system and how to develop one. Some of our basic assumptions about support systems are:

—Few clergy have a good peer support group where the trust level is high and the sharing is significant.

—Even though there is a lot of talk about clergy support groups, few clergy have acquired the skills necessary to establish a group for themselves.

—Most clergy underestimate the effect a transition will have on their lives; hence, they do not do their homework in advance to prepare to build a support system prior to a move.

—Most of us assume that good support systems happen by accident; hence, we don't intentionally set out to do the hard work required to get a good system underway.

—In start-up situations clergy need a variety of support systems; each separate system is set up to meet a specific need.

Speaking symbolically, a good support system offers us two things—blankets and sandpaper. A good support community should offer us protection and affirmation at certain times in our lives, as well as rubbing us the wrong way if that is what we need to be pushed to our growing edge again. Viewed another way, a good support system contains equal amounts of force for change and force for stability. When there's an excess of either, we suffer proportionately. Too often we erroneously think of support only in "blanket" terms (offering only affirmation, caring, and protection).

Stated still another way, a good support system contains three elements:

1. Survival—helping us get out of trouble
2. Stability—giving us a sense of continuity of values and tradition.
3. Prodding—getting us moving when we've become lazy and complacent and need to begin struggling with issues again, both internally and externally.

The next chart, entitled "The Composition of Support Systems," was designed by Dr. Charles Seashore.* It isolates the variety of our needs along with relevant types of support meeting those needs. Take a minute to review the chart.

---

*Charles Seashore, Ph.D., Social Psychologist, National Training Laboratories, Arlington, VA

THE COMPOSITION OF SUPPORT SYSTEMS

Charles Seashore

NEED	RELEVANT TYPE OF SUPPORT	SOLUTION
Confusion about future	Models	Clarity
Social	Referent group	Social
Isolation share Integration	identify;	concerns
Personal		
Isolation	Close Friends	Intimacy
	(Crisis)	Caring
Vulnerability	Helpers who can be depended on in a crisis	Assistance
Low self-esteem	Respecters of my competence	Higher esteem
Stimulus isolation and deprivation	Challengers	Perspective Energy
Environmental isolation (resources unknown)	Referral agents	Connect with

Most persons who have moved from one location to another will identify with the these needs on the chart: Social Isolation, Personal Isolation, Vulnerability, and Environmental Isolation (resources unknown).

While it is possible to seek out a separate support unit to meet each specific need listed here, we would recommend combining these needs into three separate systems:

1. One system, consisting of carefully selected parishioners, would deal with your relationships and effectiveness within the parish.
2. One, consisting of community resource persons, would deal with social and environmental issues.
3. One system would deal with personal isolation, loneliness, and vulnerability. It would be made of up highly trusted persons of your choosing.

Perhaps you're thinking that it's unrealistic to establish three separate support systems in a new parish setting. Perhaps so, but this exercise at least should encourage you to be more intentional about support systems and put some effort into designing a group or groups that can help you at this juncture. You may find that one of these three groups is already alive and active in the new place. It only takes two or three people.

More than likely you have already begun this task unconsciously. Now raise your consciousness and consider the difference between settling for some obvious resources and intentionally bringing together just the right people for these three important areas of your life.

Let's look at them one at a time.

The first kind of support structure is *a personal congregational support group*. No doubt you will be working immediately to establish a support base for yourself within the parish. A good place to begin is with the parish's official decision-making group. Next, develop credibility among your parishioners so that they will accept you as an authentic, trustworthy person in their midst.

Remember, when we talk about congregational support groups, we don't mean the kind of support the congregation as a whole provides. We are talking about a small group, three or four at most, with whom you can share your joys and difficulties during the start-up time. These people should be able to give you solid feedback regarding how you are being received and perceived.

Based on our research on pastoral start ups, we think it's difficult to receive accurate information from the parish on how you're doing. People tend to "suspend judgment" in the first few months. You may do or say things that upset or offend people, but they won't say so because they want to give you every chance to succeed. Yet their honest feedback is essential to your ability to remain open and responsive.

This is another good reason to find a small group who will tell it like it is. In addition, you will need a safe place where you can share the impact of this new parish on you. You may want to share some of this with your Board/Vestry/Session/Council. But it may be unwise strategically to "let it all hang out" with the leadership. A more informal and personal group is the better outlet. These people will be in the best position to help you alter your start-up patterns.

Here are some criteria for selecting this handful of people for your personal parish support group:

—they should be willing and able to handle vulnerable personal information discreetly;
—they should not currently be in any offfficial decision-making position in the parish;
—they should, however, have intimate knowledge of the parish and be highly respected.

You should inform your Board that you are forming this group and who will be in it. But be sure to request that the group not be connected officially to the Board or be required to report to any body. When sensitive information arises concerning you, it can be fed to one of the people in your support group.

Some denominations recommend the use of a Pastor/Parish Relations Committee in the local parish. Such a group is fine if it meets the above criteria. If you don't know who to select, try looking in these two places:

a. ex-board chairpersons not now serving in an official capacity
b. your call or search committee, people who are highly invested in your success and who probably know you better than anyone else in the parish.

One pastor we know met with his personal parish support group, made up of three persons, from 5:00 to 5:45 p.m. every Thursday for the first six months of his ministry. Because it was scheduled between work and dinner, the group did not require an extra evening meeting. Yet the pastor was able to share his thoughts and feelings and get valuable feedback on a regular basis.

Now to the second kind of support structure you should be setting up: *a support base dealing with social and environmental isolation*:

Your new community contains many of the life support systems upon which you and your family will depend during your tenure. In addition, if you wish your new parish to be accountable to its immediate environment, you need accurate information about what's out there.

Using the Hallett Model* for community analysis, you need to obtain some straight information in five important areas of community life.

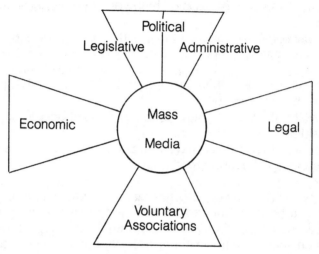

In the best of all possible worlds, it would be good to have someone representing each of these areas of community life in your support group. Such a group could help you deal with the following questions:

—where are the places in which the most human suffering
    seems to occur?
—where is there a lack of accountability in this community?
—what are the distinctive features of this community?
—who are the persons or groups that seem to control life in
    this community?

---

*Dr. Stanley Hallett, "The Sector Model" Action-Research from *A New Style of Politics, Education and Ministry*, Parker J. Palmer and Elden Jacobson, Department of Higher Education, National Council of Churches, 1971, 475 Riverside Drive, New York, NY 10027.

—how are the church and clergy viewed in this area?
—what are the key social/political/economic issues needing attention?

As you can see, questions of this sort probably are quite difficult to answer. Unless surrounded by people they trust, most individuals will be reluctant to comment. It is important to do some team-building before launching into an agenda of this kind.

Yet answers to these questions could be immensely helpful to you during this early phase of your ministry. In addition to providing important information, your group members may be able to open some doors for you to other sources of information and influence.

As a way of getting this particular group going, you may ask them to assist you while you are still relatively isolated. Try testing with this group a variety of resources they would recommend for the following:

—competent medical help for you and your family
—good schools
—competent dental care
—suitable legal and financial advice
—competent and concerned counselors, for you and your family if the need arises, and for referral purposes if members of the congregation require help
—recreational facilities and opportunities
—reliable automobile repair facilities
—assistance for the elderly, the retarded, the handicapped
—honest real estate assistance
—valued volunteer agencies
—continuing education opportunities
—specific shopping needs

More than likely members of the group will disagree about which resources are best. Just listen in on their discussion while they trade tips and advice.

Once you have established personal associations with some of the recommended resources, these community contacts can take over some dimensions of your community support group.

Now the third kind of support system: *a personal support group dealing with loneliness, vulnerability, and personal isolation.*

Clergy, their spouses, and their children feel profound loneliness after a move. They've left behind beloved friends and find it difficult to relate to people in the new situation. This loneliness can affect clergy spouses and families much more than clergy themselves. You're able to dig into your work immediately and establish contacts with people. Your spouse and children may not have that same opportunity. Some psychologists suggest that moves should be timed during the school year when your children will be able to make contact quickly with their peers.

Clergy should not, however, underestimate the impact of loneliness upon their own lives. When Hugh Eichelberger,* a Presbyterian clergyperson, made a transition from a parish to a national staff position, he took time to transcribe his impressions:

> In my own personal experience, I do not think that I took seriously enough my own grief, and I did not locate adequate pastoral care for myself. The result was that I took some unresolved grief with me into my new work that had to be dealt with after the fact in an inappropriate context. Because I was moving to a new job that did not include a manse, it was necessary for me to locate a house to buy in the area of my new work. This caused the movement of my family to be delayed for nearly two months. In retrospect, I believe that the grief process would have been facilitated if my family had been able to move away from the community at the same time I began my new work. Because they were there I had occasion to be back in the community from time to time on the weekends and this was not only confusing for those who encountered me there, but it was also confusing for me. In looking back on the experience, I suspect my delay in relocating had something to do with a desire to hold on to the experience and in a refusal to let go of that which had been particularly meaningful to me.

To deal with personal isolation and vulnerability, clergy need to establish quickly caring relationships in the new situation. To do this, you need to be looking in the right places. A good place to start is with your peers and colleagues. Check out the clergy within your own system first. Then try the ecumenical scene. There may be a group already in existence which you can join.

Next, look for mature, understanding, and caring persons within the community. To find such people, it's a good idea to join some organization that shows some promise of putting you in touch, such as:

—registering for a course at a local community college or YMCA

*Hugh L. Eichelberger, *Case Study: Ministerial Closure,* Division of Professional Development, Presbyterian Church, USA.

—joining the Rotary, Kiwanis, etc.
—joining a tennis or sports club

It's important that you make good judgments about people. It requires the skills of:

1. listening and observing
   —trying to identify the people you can trust
   —looking for points of integrity in people
   —trying to identify those persons who have a sense of humor about themselves.
2. reality testing
   —watching to see if people are shocked when you share
   —something of yourself or your ideas
   —going deeper by sharing concerns which aren't at a real gut-level
3. seed planting
   —checking to see if your contacts have ever thought of being part of a personal support system
4. pulling a group together
   —inviting the persons you've selected to an exploratory meeting
   —continuing to be straight and clear about your needs and inviting others to do the same
   —agreeing on a test-period of time, following which the process will be evaluated. (You may ask this group if it would be a personal support system for you for a limited period of time to help you through the transitional experience).

You'll need time to develop such a personal support system for yourself in your new location; During the interim, you may want to retain contact with your old support system in your former location, if distances are not prohibitive. Ask them to meet with you several times while you are getting yourself established in your new parish.

The following chart may help you become clear about your specific needs for a personal support system. You may wish to revise the listing of sources of support on the top row to make it more relevant to your situation. Be sure to ask two questions: "Do I do this for others?" and "Do they do this for me?" Draw a diagonal line through each square and answer either "yes" or "no" on both sides of the line.

SUPPORT SYSTEMS

PERSONS WHO SUPPORT ME IN MY MINISTRY DO THESE THINGS	ESSENTIAL						OTHER
	PERSONAL			PROFESSIONAL			
	SELF	FAMILY	CO-WORKERS	PEERS	ADMIN.	FRIENDS	OTHER PROFESSIONALS
Level with me							
Care enough to hold me accountable							
Let me be real							
Ask me difficult questions							
Enjoy me							
Give me a sense of my own worth & integrity							
Help me to live into the pain of being different, alone, isolated							
Affirm that I am competent & allow me to ask for help							
Call forth the best that is in me, evoking my gifts							

Once you have completed this chart, think through the steps you need to take to develop a personal support group for yourself. The chart should help you decide which elements of support you need to go after.

There are two more activities to complete before concluding this section on support systems. Both are designed to give you greater clarity on the broader support systems you have at your disposal outside this new setting. For example, most of us have family, relatives, and friends scattered in various locations, and peers and colleagues from former associations. Reflect on this broader support system and review it using the following exercise. Perhaps you can improve it through some intentional work on your part.

Take a sheet of paper and draw a large circle in the middle. Draw a small circle in the middle of the larger one to represent you.

1) This spot is reserved for people within your support system whom you want to kick out.

2) These are the people whom you want to draw into your support system.

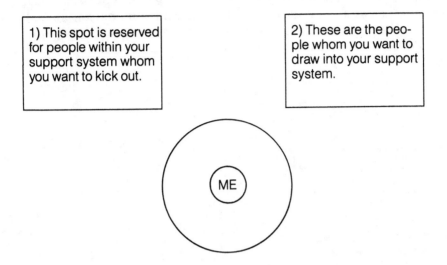

In the circle write the names of the people who currently constitute your broader support community. Include here everyone from spouse and relatives to professional associates. Place those closest to you nearest to the center of the circle. Enclose them in a larger circle than the others. Once you feel you have included all the persons significant to you, begin to critique the value of these persons to you based on the kind of support system you currently need or will need during the transitional period. More than likely, you will observe that some people are toxic to your life and should not be included. These persons should be shifted with an arrow to space number 1.

As you reflect on the kind of people you need in order to have a balanced system, begin to list those new people in space number 2. Draw them into your support circle by means of an arrow. Place them as near or as far from you as seems appropriate. Think through what it would take to draw them within your support circle. What pay off is there for them to want to do this for you?

One final exercise will help you focus on possible shifts you may need to make to balance your support needs. Draw two pie-graphs which represent the totality of your support needs. One graph will represent those needs as they currently are divided among people and institutions. The second graph represents what you consider a more ideal spread of needs. If you find considerable difference between the ideal and the actual, take a minute now to plan steps you will take to move from one to the other.

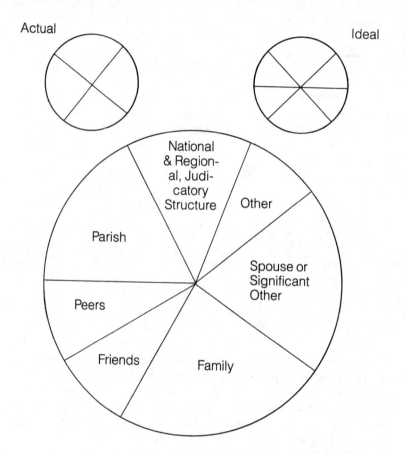

Actual

Ideal

National & Region-al, Judi-catory Structure

Other

Parish

Spouse or Significant Other

Peers

Friends

Family

Feedback

We discovered early in our research on pastoral start ups that there is no such thing as a honeymoon period. What might feel like a honeymoon for clergy is really a period of "suspended judgment." But make no mistake—people are watching you very carefully and making judgments all the time. They may not verbalize these opinions directly to you because they really do want to "give you a chance." In fact, during this period of suspended judgment, your parishioners may actually be giving you enough rope to hang yourself. Even though you may be doing or saying things that offend, annoy, or hurt parishioners, you may never know it and feel, wrongly, that all is well.

For this reason we recommend setting in motion a process for getting accurate information on the effects of your ministry during the start-up period. One process, sharing surprises, was described in Chapter 5. Another is called *planned renegotiation,** more popularly called "The Pinch Theory." It allows both pastor and congregation to register their need to renegotiate the relationship if the present way of relating results in a *pinch* for someone.

Studies indicate that social systems progress through a natural cycle which begins with the needs of persons and/or organizations. Within church systems, a congregation tries as best it can to define its need for pastoral leadership. Clergy in turn try to express as best they can their skills and abilities to serve, along with their needs and wants. Out of these negotiations a pastor and congregation commit themselves to an agreement/covenant/contract/promise.

After the negotiation, a period of productive work usually follows. Both pastor and congregation work together in a stable way.

Inevitably, however, there is a *disruption* which is part of the natural cycle of human work relationships. Even with the best of negotiated contracts, disruption will occur because in a dynamic situation people change and organizations change. Change is inevitable if real human beings are involved.

Following are some other reasons why disruption will inevitably occur:

1. The inability to initially share all expectations
2. The presence of values and styles which were not seen earlier
3. The belief that "we can change them" afterwards
4. Changes in the external environment of congregation, community, family, etc.
5. Internal changes in people and congregations.

When these factors are introduced into an established relationship, disruption will result. When this disruption or "pinch" occurs, a time of anxiety and uncertainty comes rushing in and results in three responses:

---

*John J. Sherwood and John C. Glidewell, *Planned Renegotiation: A Norm-Setting OD Intervention*, The 1973 Annual Handbook for Group Facilitators.

1. The natural reaction is to return to "the way it was." That is, we ignore or discard the "new information" that impelled itself into the relationship. The drive for this response is strong, but it is a trap. In most cases the "new information" will have its way—often in more intense and spectacular manner—unless dealt with rationally.

2. Termination is a radical but acceptable response. If the situation is such that the covenant can no longer be honored, it is then reasonable and just to part. This sounds easier than it is, but it is always an option. Termination is not necessarily failure. It does mean things have changed. Failure, incidentally, is also "okay."

3. Renegotiation is the process of going through all the steps that got us into the disruption. We return to identifying the needs, sharing information, and making a new commitment.

The social systems process is significant because it encourages us to expect disruptions as natural occurrences and make plans to utilize them in renewing the ministry of congregation and leader. One way to do this is by regularly sharing with one another those "missed expectations" or changes in person or environment when they come up. In the social system these are the "pinches." If we heed these early warning signs, we may be able to make "in-ministry adjustments" rather than let problems pile up so that they necessitate major renegotiations.

The visual below illustrates this social system process:

PLANNED RENEGOTIATION

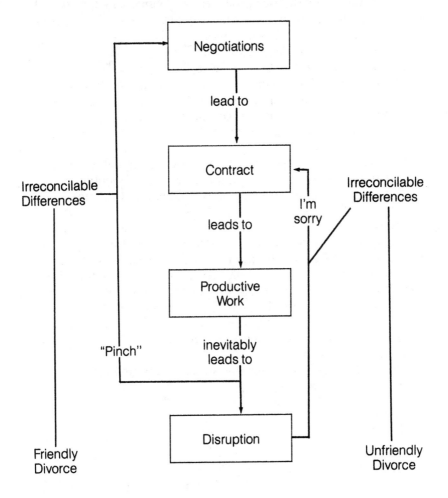

Among the various norms you may want to establish in this new congregation, one should be the ability to renegotiate relationships when "pinches" occur. This norm, when established, will continually allow for readjustment in the kind and type of interaction between you and the congregation.

We do not recommend that this negotiation and renegotiation process be formalized into an actual work contract—at least not in the initial stage of ministry. (An exception is salary, housing, and other allowances.) Both pastor and congregation know too little about each other to be establishing a viable working covenant.

However, we do affirm the validity of such a covenant later—perhaps after the 12-month mark. In establishing the contract or covenant, be sure to include the possibility of planned renegotiation if either you or the congregation feels a "pinch."

CHAPTER XIII

Writing Your Own Obituary

Writing your obituary at this juncture in your life may seem like a strange activity. You are about to begin another chapter in your life with this new parish; why interject such a somber note?

It will be worth your energy to do so simply as a values-clarification exercise. As this should not take you more than 20 minutes, it will be time well spent. We include this exercise to help you be clearer about what you want to do with your life. Before your life becomes consumed with new activities and demands, it's important for you to affirm your basic reason for being in this new situation. Where is it that you want your life to count? What parts of your ministry do you want to be remembered for?

Simply write in the appropriate paragraphs. It should read like a newspaper article written at the time of your death.

_____ died today at the age of _____.

She/he is survived

by _____.

She/he will be remembered

by _____.

Mr./Mrs. _____ was noted for _____

_____

_____. She/he was the type of person

who

_____. His/her

significant accomplishments

included _____

_____. At the

time of death, she/he was deeply engaged

in _____

_____.

How does it read? By and large, do you feel satisfied with the way your life is going? You may decide that you want to be different in the future. If so, now is the time to plan for that change. Outline the differences you wish to make in your life before moving on to other tasks.

CHAPTER XIV

Dialogue With the Congregation

The following procedure is adapted from the work of Ira Progoff, the author-teacher of *The Intensive Journal*. He contends that one way of staying in touch with oneself and one's life journey is to carry on a dialogue with one's work. In the Alban Institute's clergy transition seminars we often make use of this technique because it helps pastors get more fully in touch with a new congregation and identify potential difficulties down the line. The technique will help clarify the psychological contract you and the parish have with each other. It also gets at the frustration many clergy feel when they want to have a dialogue with the entire parish. Who can really speak for the parish in this regard? No one. Hence one needs to carry out the dialogue in another fashion.

The exercise requires that you first spend some time dealing with the history of the parish (as described in Chapter 6). The historizing process will give you a sense of the *personality* of the congregation—those characteristics and traits that together make a whole impression.

Begin thinking of the parish as a single unit with whom you can carry on a dialogue. Once you have the parish fixed in your mind, begin writing out the dialogue on a pad of paper. Try not to think about this process too much. Allow the dialogue to carry itself. Simply begin by saying something to the parish. Then have the parish respond. Then you answer that response. And so on.

Do the dialogue in one sitting. Allow yourself to be carried away by the experience. Don't go back to re-read or critique the experience until you finish. You may be surprised at where it takes you.

The experience won't seem so artificial once you get into it. Do it! See what learnings come forth.

Then share the dialogue with a friend or trusted parishioner.

Some of the clergy in our seminars have taken this piece of writing back to their official boards for their reactions.

Endings and Beginnings

This is the ending of a book on new beginnings. I hope you have gained a new sense of the importance of endings and beginnings. The way you end and the way you begin will be a genuine expression of who you are and how deeply you care for people. Without some intentionality on how we exit and enter systems, those old self-defeating patterns may communicate to others a lack of caring.

It is my hope that this workbook will help all of us church professionals bring to our endings and beginnings a new dimension of professional effectiveness.